Unity Multiplayer Games

Build engaging, fully functional, multiplayer games with
Unity engine

Alan R. Stagner

BIRMINGHAM - MUMBAI

Unity Multiplayer Games

First published: December 2013

Production Reference: 2251113

Published by Packt Publishing Ltd.
Livery Place
35 Livery Street
Birmingham B3 2PB, UK.

ISBN 978-1-84969-232-8

www.packtpub.com

Cover Image by Prashant Timappa Shetty (sparkling.spectrum.123@gmail.com)

Credits

Author
Alan R. Stagner

Reviewers
Clifford Champion
Fabio Ferrara
Sriram. A. S.

Acquisition Editor
Rubal Kaur

Lead Technical Editor
Madhuja Chaudhari

Technical Editors
Dipika Gaonkar
Mrunmayee Patil

Project Coordinator
Apeksha Chitnis

Proofreader
Linda Morris

Indexer
Hemangini Bari

Graphics
Abhinash Sahu

Production Coordinator
Alwin Roy

Cover Work
Alwin Roy

About the Author

Alan R. Stagner is an independent developer with a passion for Unity3D game development. He was introduced to programming by his father, he sought out different ways to create games in a variety of languages. Most recently, he found the Unity game engine and was instantly hooked, and discovered his love of multiplayer game development. He has also dabbled in database and server programming from time to time, mostly involving PHP and MySQL with recent forays into ASP.NET.

I'd like to thank my family and friends, of course—my father is the entire reason I'm a programmer and has helped me every step of the way. Everyone I know has been incredibly supportive. I'd like to thank the Unity community—without them I don't think I would know Unity like I do today. I'd also like to thank Unity for providing such an awesome platform and making it so easy for me to write my first multiplayer game.

About the Reviewers

Clifford Champion has a broad background in software engineering, with years of experience spanning 3D games and Internet applications, and more recently in machine learning. He holds a degree in Mathematics from UCLA. In the past, he has worked as an integration and support engineer at Havok, and also as a lead interactive media and Internet apps programmer at PlainJoe Studios.

Now, he works for zSpace (zspace.com), a hardware/software company creating highly immersive, interactive 3D displays for classrooms, industry, and entertainment. At zSpace, he is a member of the software platform team, helping to enable the holographic-like experience on a variety of game engines and platforms, including Unity. Clifford can be found on Twitter at @duckmaestro and welcomes any discussions.

Fabio Ferrara is a game developer. He is working for Chubby Pixel, an independent game studio based in Milan, which he founded in 2012. They work thoroughly to bring to the users the best possible gaming experience. He has also collaborated for the publication of other books such as *Unity iOS Essentials*, *Packt Publishing*.

Sriram. A. S. is a software developer who is currently living in Pune, India. He works primarily in C/C++ and Java. He has been working with Unity 3D from its very early versions; and has developed codes related to its integration with features such as augmented reality, and shared them on his tech blog (http://mypersonalsoft.blogspot.com).

In his spare time, he works on a few open source software. And he also likes to experiment with various other technologies and ideas, along with his team of code passionate friends — the "Hobby Coders" (http://hobbycoders.com).

www.PacktPub.com

Support files, eBooks, discount offers, and more

You might want to visit www.packtpub.com for support files and downloads related to your book.

Did you know that Packt offers eBook versions of every book published, with PDF and ePub files available? You can upgrade to the eBook version at www.packtpub.com and as a print book customer, you are entitled to a discount on the eBook copy. Get in touch with us at service@packtpub.com for more details.

At www.packtpub.com, you can also read a collection of free technical articles, sign up for a range of free newsletters and receive exclusive discounts and offers on Packt books and eBooks.

http://PacktLib.PacktPub.com

Do you need instant solutions to your IT questions? PacktLib is Packt's online digital book library. Here, you can access, read and search across Packt's entire library of books.

Why Subscribe?
- Fully searchable across every book published by Packt
- Copy and paste, print and bookmark content
- On demand and accessible via web browser

Free Access for Packt account holders

If you have an account with Packt at www.packtpub.com, you can use this to access PacktLib today and view nine entirely free books. Simply use your login credentials for immediate access.

Table of Contents

Preface

This book intends to step you through the concepts and middleware involved in creating multiplayer games with the Unity game engine. I've been a big fan of multiplayer games for a while. They have a way of tapping into our basic desires, fulfilling a need to compete, to co-operate, and most of all to socialize with our fellow humans, in a way that no single player game can ever provide.

I've experienced a wide range of networking plugins and applications in Unity. As I learn new networking systems, there are always stumbling blocks and difficult issues. I wrote this book because I wanted to help others on the same path, and help them surmount the issues I encountered myself.

Unity IDE crash course

To better understand this book, we'll need to cover the basic features of the Unity IDE.

If you open Unity for the first time, you'll be presented with a window where you can either open an existing project or create a new one. Select the **Create New Project** tab, and choose a location for your project.

Once your project is created, you'll see a number of panels. There are the **Scene** and **Game** tabs, the **Hierarchy**, **Project**, and **Console** tabs, and the **Inspector** tab.

The **Scene** view shows the current scene. This will allow you to navigate the scene, select objects, move them around, and more. The **Game** view shows the view of the main camera. If you press the **Play** button, the **Game** view is automatically shown and allows you to play test your game from inside the editor.

The **Hierarchy** tab shows the object hierarchy of the current scene. This allows you to select objects, parent or unparent them, delete them, rename them, and much more.

The **Inspector** tab shows the editors for each component attached to the selected object (rather than being inheritance based like many traditional engines, Unity is component based, where objects are a collection of components and each component has a separate responsibility). It allows you to set values and change properties of components. You can also remove components by right clicking on a component and clicking on **Remove Component**. In Unity 4 and later, you can also click on the **Add Component** button and select a component script.

The **Project** tab shows the assets in your project. You can drop game assets here to import them, and you can create new materials, scripts, and shaders by right-clicking and selecting the **Create** option. You can also drag objects from the **Hierarchy** to the **Project** tab to create a **prefab**. Prefabs are essentially object templates—you can **Instantiate** a prefab to create an exact copy of the prefab in the scene (for instance, you might create an Enemy prefab, and instantiate it to spawn enemies). You can also drag component scripts from the Project to the Inspector of a selected game object to add the component to the object.

To learn more about Unity, you can get started here:

```
http://unity3d.com/learn
```

What this book covers

Chapter 1, Unity Networking – The Pong Game, introduces the concept of reliable UDP communication, and different types of servers employed by games. It covers Unity Networking, and creating a networked two-player Pong clone.

Chapter 2, Photon Unity Networking – The Chat Client, covers a third-party alternative to Unity Networking. It introduces the concept of the cloud-hosted game servers, simple matchmaking, and friends lists. It also covers the creation of a simple chat client.

Chapter 3, Photon Server – Star Collector, introduces dedicated servers for games. It covers creating a Photon Server application, connecting to a server, using the request/response/event system to communicate, and creating a simple Star Collector game.

Chapter 4, Player.IO – Bot Wars, covers an alternative dedicated server system. It introduces the database features of Player.IO, how to create a Player.IO server, connecting from Unity, and creating a simple RTS-style game with persistent user stats.

Chapter 5, PubNub – The Global Chatbox, introduces communication over an HTTP messaging service. It covers benefits and pitfalls of HTTP for communication, using the WWW class to communicate via PubNub, and creating a chatroom application.

Chapter 6, Entity Interpolation and Prediction, introduces the concept of server-side movement physics and potential issues and solutions. It covers client-side movement prediction, and how to smooth the motion of remote entities.

Chapter 7, Server-side Hit Detection, introduces the concept of server-side hit detection for shooter-style games. It covers the reasons behind target-leading problems in many online games, and how to resolve the issue by rewinding the game state.

What you need for this book

You will need Unity 3 or later for this book. Many chapters require specific downloads:

- *Chapter 2, Photon Unity Networking – The Chat Client*, requires the Photon Unity Networking plugin
- *Chapter 3, Photon Server – Star Collector*, requires the Photon Server client and server SDKs
- *Chapter 4, Player.IO – Bot Wars*, requires the Player.IO developer package
- *Chapter 5, PubNub – The Global Chatbox*, requires a third-party JSON parser

Instructions to download the required materials are covered at the beginning of each chapter.

Who this book is for

This book is for developers who want to get started writing multiplayer games with the Unity game engine. Readers are expected to have a working knowledge of C#. Knowledge of the Unity IDE is helpful, but not strictly required.

Conventions

In this book, you will find a number of styles of text that distinguish between different kinds of information. Here are some examples of these styles, and an explanation of their meaning.

Code words in text are shown as follows: "Navigate to the Release folder and run the EXE."

A block of code is set as follows:

```
public class ExampleUnityNetworkSerializePosition : MonoBehaviour
{
  public void OnSerializeNetworkView( BitStream stream,
    NetworkMessageInfo info )
  {
    // we are currently writing information to the network
    if( stream.isWriting )
    {
      // send the object's position
      Vector3 position = transform.position;
      stream.Serialize( ref position );
    }
  }
```

When we wish to draw your attention to a particular part of a code block, the relevant lines or items are set in bold:

```
// the maximum score a player can reach
public int ScoreLimit = 10;

// the display test for player 1's score
public TextMesh Player1ScoreDisplay;

// the display text for player 2's score
public TextMesh Player2ScoreDisplay;

// Player 1's score
private int p1Score = 0;
```

New terms and **important words** are shown in bold. Words that you see on the screen, in menus, or dialog boxes for example, appear in the text like this: "clicking the **Next** button moves you to the next screen".

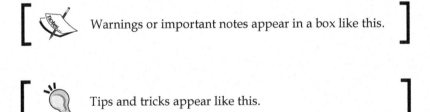

Warnings or important notes appear in a box like this.

Tips and tricks appear like this.

Reader feedback

Feedback from our readers is always welcome. Let us know what you think about this book—what you liked or may have disliked. Reader feedback is important for us to develop titles that you really get the most out of.

To send us general feedback, simply send an e-mail to feedback@packtpub.com, and mention the book title via the subject of your message.

If there is a topic that you have expertise in and you are interested in either writing or contributing to a book, see our author guide on www.packtpub.com/authors.

Customer support

Now that you are the proud owner of a Packt book, we have a number of things to help you to get the most from your purchase.

Downloading the example code

You can download the example code files for all Packt books you have purchased from your account at http://www.packtpub.com. If you purchased this book elsewhere, you can visit http://www.packtpub.com/support and register to have the files e-mailed directly to you.

Errata

Although we have taken every care to ensure the accuracy of our content, mistakes do happen. If you find a mistake in one of our books—maybe a mistake in the text or the code—we would be grateful if you would report this to us. By doing so, you can save other readers from frustration and help us improve subsequent versions of this book. If you find any errata, please report them by visiting http://www.packtpub.com/submit-errata, selecting your book, clicking on the **errata submission form** link, and entering the details of your errata. Once your errata are verified, your submission will be accepted and the errata will be uploaded on our website, or added to any list of existing errata, under the Errata section of that title. Any existing errata can be viewed by selecting your title from http://www.packtpub.com/support.

Piracy

Piracy of copyright material on the Internet is an ongoing problem across all media. At Packt, we take the protection of our copyright and licenses very seriously. If you come across any illegal copies of our works, in any form, on the Internet, please provide us with the location address or website name immediately so that we can pursue a remedy.

Please contact us at copyright@packtpub.com with a link to the suspected pirated material.

We appreciate your help in protecting our authors, and our ability to bring you valuable content.

Questions

You can contact us at questions@packtpub.com if you are having a problem with any aspect of the book, and we will do our best to address it.

1
Unity Networking – The Pong Game

Multiplayer is everywhere. It's a staple of AAA games and small-budget indie offerings alike. Multiplayer games tap into our most basic human desires. Whether it be teaming up with strangers to survive a zombie apocalypse, or showing off your skills in a round of "Capture the Flag" on your favorite map, no artificial intelligence in the world comes close to the feeling of playing with a living, breathing, and thinking human being.

Unity3D has a sizable number of third-party networking middleware aimed at developing multiplayer games, and is arguably one of the easiest platforms to prototype multiplayer games.

The first networking system most people encounter in Unity is the built-in **Unity Networking API**. This API simplifies a great many tasks in writing networked code by providing a framework for networked objects rather than just sending messages. This works by providing a NetworkView component, which can serialize object state and call functions across the network.

Additionally, Unity provides a Master server, which essentially lets players search among all public servers to find a game to join, and can also help players in connecting to each other from behind private networks.

In this chapter, we will cover:

- Introducing multiplayer
- Introducing UDP communication
- Setting up your own Master server for testing
- What a NetworkView is

- Serializing object state
- Calling RPCs
- Starting servers and connecting to them
- Using the Master server API to register servers and browse available hosts
- Setting up a dedicated server model
- Loading networked levels
- Creating a Pong clone using Unity networking

Introducing multiplayer games

Before we get started on the details of communication over the Internet, what exactly does multiplayer entail in a game?

As far as most players are concerned, in a multiplayer game they are sharing the same experience with other players. It looks and feels like they are playing the same game. In reality, they aren't. Each player is playing a separate game, each with its own game state. Trying to ensure that all players are playing the exact same game is prohibitively expensive. Instead, games attempt to synchronize just enough information to give the illusion of a shared experience.

Games are almost ubiquitously built around a client-server architecture, where each client connects to a single server. The server is the main hub of the game, ideally the machine for processing the game state, although at the very least it can serve as a simple "middleman" for messages between clients. Each client represents an instance of the game running on a computer. In some cases the server might also have a client, for instance some games allow you to host a game without starting up an external server program.

While an **MMO (Massively Multiplayer Online)** might directly connect to one of these servers, many games do not have prior knowledge of the server IPs. For example, FPS games often let players host their own servers. In order to show the user a list of servers they can connect to, games usually employ another server, known as the "Master Server" or alternatively the "Lobby server". This server's sole purpose is to keep track of game servers which are currently running, and report a list of these to clients. Game servers connect to the Master server in order to announce their presence publicly, and game clients query the Master server to get an updated list of game servers currently running.

Alternatively, this Master server sometimes does not keep track of servers at all. Sometimes games employ "matchmaking", where players connect to the Lobby server and list their criteria for a game. The server places this player in a "bucket" based on their criteria, and whenever a bucket is full enough to start a game, a host is chosen from these players and that client starts up a server in the background, which the other players connect to. This way, the player does not have to browse servers manually and can instead simply tell the game what they want to play.

Introducing UDP communication

The built-in Unity networking is built upon **RakNet**. RakNet uses UDP communication for efficiency.

UDP (User Datagram Protocols) is a simple way to send messages to another computer. These messages are largely unchecked, beyond a simple checksum to ensure that the message has not been corrupted. Because of this, messages are not guaranteed to arrive, nor are they guaranteed to only arrive once (occasionally a single message can be delivered twice or more), or even in any particular order. TCP, on the other hand, guarantees each message to be received just once, and in the exact order they were sent, although this can result in increased latency (messages must be resent several times if they fail to reach the target, and messages must be buffered when received, in order to be processed in the exact order they were sent).

To solve this, a reliability layer must be built on top of UDP. This is known as **rUDP** (**reliable UDP**). Messages can be sent unreliably (they may not arrive, or may arrive more than once), or reliably (they are guaranteed to arrive, only once per message, and in the correct order). If a reliable message was not received or was corrupt, the original sender has to resend the message. Additionally, messages will be stored rather than immediately processed if they are not in order. For example, if you receive messages 1, 2, and 4, your program will not be able to handle those messages until message 3 arrives.

Allowing unreliable or reliable switching on a per-message basis affords better overall performance. Messages, such as player position, are better suited to unreliable messages (if one fails to arrive, another one will arrive soon anyway), whereas damage messages must be reliable (you never want to accidentally drop a damage message, and having them arrive in the same order they were sent reduces race conditions).

In Unity, you can serialize the state of an object (for example, you might serialize the position and health of a unit) either reliably or unreliably (unreliable is usually preferred). All other messages are sent reliably.

Setting up the Master Server

Although Unity provide their own default Master Server and Facilitator (which is connected automatically if you do not specify your own), it is not recommended to use this for production. We'll be using our own Master Server, so you know how to connect to one you've hosted yourself.

Firstly, go to the following page:

`http://unity3d.com/master-server/`

We're going to download two of the listed server components: the **Master Server** and the **Facilitator** as shown in the following screenshot:

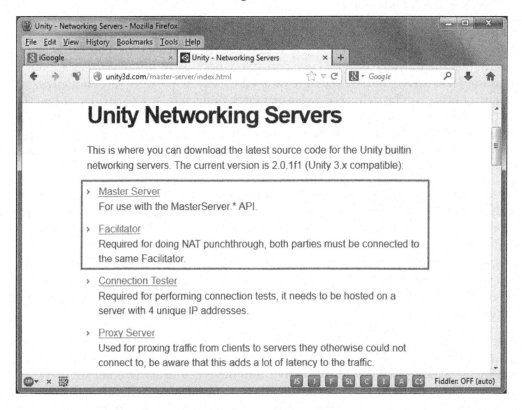

The servers are provided in full source, zipped. If you are on Windows using Visual Studio Express, open up the Visual Studio .sln solution and compile in the **Release** mode. Navigate to the `Release` folder and run the EXE (`MasterServer.exe` or `Facilitator.exe`). If you are on a Mac, you can either use the included XCode project, or simply run the Makefile (the Makefile works under both Linux and Mac OS X).

The Master Server, as previously mentioned, enables our game to show a server lobby to players. The Facilitator is used to help clients connect to each other by performing an operation known as **NAT punch-through**. NAT is used when multiple computers are part of the same network, and all use the same public IP address. NAT will essentially translate public and private IPs, but in order for one machine to connect to another, NAT punch-through is necessary. You can read more about it here:

http://www.raknet.net/raknet/manual/natpunchthrough.html

The default port for the Master Server is 23466, and for the Facilitator is 50005. You'll need these later in order to configure Unity to connect to the local Master Server and Facilitator instead of the default Unity-hosted servers.

Now that we've set up our own servers, let's take a look at the Unity Networking API itself.

NetworkViews and state serialization

In Unity, game objects that need to be networked have a **NetworkView** component. The NetworkView component handles communication over the network, and even helps make networked state serialization easier. It can automatically serialize the state of a Transform, Rigidbody, or Animation component, or in one of your own scripts you can write a custom serialization function.

When attached to a game object, NetworkView will generate a NetworkViewID for NetworkView. This ID serves to uniquely identify a NetworkView across the network. An object can be saved as part of a scene with NetworkView attached (this can be used for game managers, chat boxes, and so on), or it can be saved in the project as a prefab and spawned later via Network.Instantiate (this is used to generate player objects, bullets, and so on). Network.Instantiate is the multiplayer equivalent to GameObject.Instantiate—it sends a message over the network to other clients so that all clients spawn the object. It also assigns a network ID to the object, which is used to identify the object across multiple clients (the same object will have the same network ID on every client).

 A prefab is a template for a game object (such as the player object). You can use the Instantiate methods to create a copy of the template in the scene.

Spawned network game objects can also be destroyed via `Network.Destroy`. It is the multiplayer counterpart of `GameObject.Destroy`. It sends a message to all clients so that they all destroy the object. It also deletes any RPC messages associated with that object.

NetworkView has a single component that it will serialize. This can be a Transform, a Rigidbody, an Animation, or one of your own components that has an `OnSerializeNetworkView` function. Serialized values can either be sent with the **ReliableDeltaCompressed** option, where values are always sent reliably and compressed to include only changes since the last update, or they can be sent with the **Unreliable** option, where values are not sent reliably and always include the full values (not the change since the last update, since that would be impossible to predict over UDP). Each method has its own advantages and disadvantages. If data is constantly changing, such as player position in a first person shooter, in general Unreliable is preferred to reduce latency. If data does not often change, use the ReliableDeltaCompressed option to reduce bandwidth (as only changes will be serialized).

NetworkView can also call methods across the network via **Remote Procedure Calls (RPC)**. RPCs are always completely reliable in Unity Networking, although some networking libraries allow you to send unreliable RPCs, such as uLink or TNet.

Writing a custom state serializer

While initially a game might simply serialize Transform or Rigidbody for testing, eventually it is often necessary to write a custom serialization function. This is a surprisingly easy task.

Downloading the example code

You can download the example code files for all Packt books you have purchased from your account at http://www.packtpub.com. If you purchased this book elsewhere, you can visit http://www.packtpub.com/support and register to have the files e-mailed directly to you.

Here is a script that sends an object's position over the network:

```
using UnityEngine;
using System.Collections;
public class ExampleUnityNetworkSerializePosition : MonoBehaviour
{
  public void OnSerializeNetworkView( BitStream stream,
    NetworkMessageInfo info )
  {
```

```
      // we are currently writing information to the network
      if( stream.isWriting )
      {
        // send the object's position
        Vector3 position = transform.position;
        stream.Serialize( ref position );
      }
      // we are currently reading information from the network
      else
      {
        // read the first vector3 and store it in 'position'
        Vector3 position = Vector3.zero;
        stream.Serialize( ref position );

        // set the object's position to the value we were sent
        transform.position = position;
      }
    }
  }
}
```

Most of the work is done with BitStream. This is used to check if NetworkView is currently writing the state, or if it is reading the state from the network. Depending on whether it is reading or writing, stream.Serialize behaves differently. If NetworkView is writing, the value will be sent over the network. However, if NetworkView is reading, the value will be read from the network and saved in the referenced variable (thus the ref keyword, which passes Vector3 by reference rather than value).

Using RPCs

RPCs are useful for single, self-contained messages that need to be sent, such as a character firing a gun, or a player saying something in chat.

In Unity, RPCs are methods marked with the [RPC] attribute. This can be called by name via networkView.RPC("methodName", ...). For example, the following script prints to the console on all machines when the space key is pressed.

```
using UnityEngine;
using System.Collections;

public class ExampleUnityNetworkCallRPC : MonoBehavior
{
  void Update()
  {
    // important - make sure not to run if this networkView is not
```

```
      ours
   if( !networkView.isMine )
     return;

   // if space key is pressed, call RPC for everybody
   if( Input.GetKeyDown( KeyCode.Space ) )
     networkView.RPC( "testRPC", RPCMode.All );
}

[RPC]
void testRPC( NetworkMessageInfo info )
{
   // log the IP address of the machine that called this RPC
   Debug.Log( "Test RPC called from " + info.sender.ipAddress );
}
}
```

Also note the use of `NetworkView.isMine` to determine ownership of an object. All scripts will run 100 percent of the time regardless of whether your machine owns the object or not, so you have to be careful to avoid letting some logic run on remote machines; for example, player input code should only run on the machine that owns the object.

RPCs can either be sent to a number of players at once, or to a specific player. You can either pass an RPCMode to specify which group of players to receive the message, or a specific NetworkPlayer to send the message to. You can also specify any number of parameters to be passed to the RPC method.

RPCMode includes the following entries:

- **All** (the RPC is called for everyone)
- **AllBuffered** (the RPC is called for everyone, and then buffered for when new players connect, until the object is destroyed)
- **Others** (the RPC is called for everyone except the sender)
- **OthersBuffered** (the RPC is called for everyone except the sender, and then buffered for when new players connect, until the object is destroyed)
- **Server** (the RPC is sent to the host machine)

 Note that, with the exception of `RPCMode.All` and `RPCMode.AllBuffered`, a client cannot send an RPC to itself.

Initializing a server

The first thing you will want to set up is hosting games and joining games. To initialize a server on the local machine, call `Network.InitializeServer`.

This method takes three parameters: the number of allowed incoming connections, the port to listen on, and whether to use NAT punch-through. The following script initializes a server on port 25000 which allows 8 clients to connect:

```
using UnityEngine;
using System.Collections;

public class ExampleUnityNetworkInitializeServer : MonoBehavior
{
  void OnGUI()
  {
    if( GUILayout.Button( "Launch Server" ) )
    {
      LaunchServer();
    }
  }

  // launch the server
  void LaunchServer()
  {
    // Start a server that enables NAT punchthrough,
    // listens on port 25000,
    // and allows 8 clients to connect
    Network.InitializeServer( 8, 25005, true );
  }

  // called when the server has been initialized
  void OnServerInitialized()
  {
    Debug.Log( "Server initialized" );
  }
}
```

You can also optionally enable an incoming password (useful for private games) by setting `Network.incomingPassword` to a password string of the player's choice, and initializing a general-purpose security layer by calling `Network.InitializeSecurity()`. Both of these should be set up before actually initializing the server.

 Note that incoming connections does not mean maximum player count, since it does not include the host (for example, if you allow 8 players to connect, it's possible for 9 players to play in the same room—8 clients plus the host).

Connecting to a server

To connect to a server you know the IP address of, you can call `Network.Connect`.

The following script allows the player to enter an IP, a port, and an optional password and attempts to connect to the server:

```
using UnityEngine;
using System.Collections;
public class ExampleUnityNetworkingConnectToServer : MonoBehavior
{
  private string ip = "";
  private string port = "";
  private string password = "";
  void OnGUI()
  {
    GUILayout.Label( "IP Address" );
    ip = GUILayout.TextField( ip, GUILayout.Width( 200f ) );
    GUILayout.Label( "Port" );
    port = GUILayout.TextField( port, GUILayout.Width( 50f ) );
    GUILayout.Label( "Password (optional)" );
    password = GUILayout.PasswordField( password, '*',
      GUILayout.Width( 200f ) );
    if( GUILayout.Button( "Connect" ) )
    {
      int portNum = 25005;
      // failed to parse port number - a more ideal solution is to
      limit input to numbers only, a number of examples can be
      found on the Unity forums
      if( !int.TryParse( port, out portNum ) )
```

```
        {
            Debug.LogWarning( "Given port is not a number" );
        }
        // try to initiate a direct connection to the server
        else
        {
            Network.Connect( ip, portNum, password );
        }
    }
}

void OnConnectedToServer()
{
    Debug.Log( "Connected to server!" );
}

void OnFailedToConnect( NetworkConnectionError error )
{
    Debug.Log( "Failed to connect to server: " +
        error.ToString() );
}

}
```

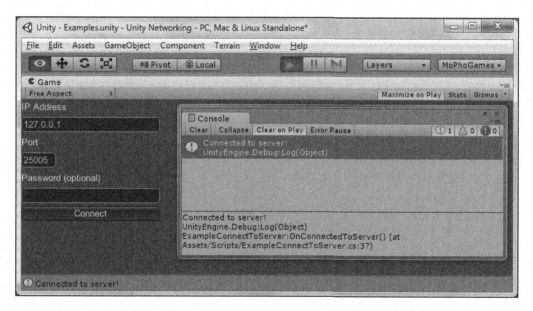

Connecting to the Master Server

While we could just allow the player to enter IP addresses to connect to servers (and many games do, such as Minecraft), it's much more convenient to allow the player to browse a list of public servers. This is what the Master Server is for.

Now that you can start up a server and connect to it, let's take a look at how to connect to the Master Server you downloaded earlier. First, make sure both the Master Server and Facilitator are running. I will assume you are running them on your local machine (IP is 127.0.0.1), but of course you can run these on a different computer and use that machine's IP address. Keep in mind, if you want the Master Server publicly accessible, it must be installed on a machine with a public IP address (it cannot be in a private network).

Let's configure Unity to use our Master Server rather than the Unity-hosted test server. The following script configures the Master Server and Facilitator to connect to a given IP (by default 127.0.0.1):

```
using UnityEngine;
using System.Collections;

public class ExampleUnityNetworkingConnectToMasterServer :
  MonoBehaviour
{
  // Assuming Master Server and Facilitator are on the same
    machine
  public string MasterServerIP = "127.0.0.1";

  void Awake()
  {
    // set the IP and port of the Master Server to connect to
    MasterServer.ipAddress = MasterServerIP;
    MasterServer.port = 23466;

    // set the IP and port of the Facilitator to connect to
    Network.natFacilitatorIP = MasterServerIP;
    Network.natFacilitatorPort = 50005;
  }
}
```

Registering a server with the Master Server

Now that you've configured the Master Server, it's time to register a server with it. This is easy to do.

Immediately after making a call to `Network.InitializeServer`, make another call to `MasterServer.RegisterHost`. This call connects to the Master Server and tells it to display our server in the public game list.

The `RegisterHost` function takes three parameters, all strings: `gameTypeName`, `gameName`, and `comment`. The game type name is used to separate different game listings from each other. For example, if two games use the same Master Server, they would both supply different game type names in order to avoid getting listings for the other game. The game name is the name of the host server, for example "John's server". The comment is a general purpose data string, essentially anything can be stored here. For example you could store data about the server (such as map rotation, available modes, and so on) and display these to the user while they browse the lobby.

Because RegisterHost is a separate call from InitializeServer, you can simply omit the call to RegisterHost to implement private or LAN-style servers.

You can call RegisterHost more than once while a server is running to update the information stored on the Master Server. For example, if the server changes to a new level, you might call RegisterHost again to update the lobby.

Browsing available servers

To browse the available servers, call `MasterServer.RequestHostList`. This takes one single parameter: the game type name (this is the same game type name you passed to RegisterHost).

This does not return anything, instead the result will be asynchronously downloaded, and the last known list of servers can be accessed via `MasterServer.PollHostList`. Additionally, to ensure you aren't using old data, you can call `MasterServer.ClearHostList`. For example, if the user hits the Refresh button in the lobby you might clear the host list and then request a new list from the Master Server.

The following script shows a lobby for users to browse available servers and connect to them:

```
using UnityEngine;
using System.Collections;

public class ExampleUnityNetworkingBrowseServers : MonoBehavior
{
  // are we currently trying to download a host list?
  private bool loading = false;

  // the current position within the scrollview
  private Vector2 scrollPos = Vector2.zero;

  void Start()
  {
    // immediately request a list of hosts
    refreshHostList();
  }

  void OnGUI()
  {
    if( GUILayout.Button( "Refresh" ) )
    {
      refreshHostList();
    }

    if( loading )
    {
      GUILayout.Label( "Loading..." );
    }
    else
    {
      scrollPos = GUILayout.BeginScrollView( scrollPos,
        GUILayout.Width( 200f ), GUILayout.Height( 200f ) );

      HostData[] hosts = MasterServer.PollHostList();
      for( int i = 0; i < hosts.Length; i++ )
      {
        if( GUILayout.Button( hosts[i].gameName,
          GUILayout.ExpandWidth( true ) ) )
        {
          Network.Connect( hosts[i] );
        }
      }
```

```
      if( hosts.Length == 0 )
      {
        GUILayout.Label( "No servers running" );
      }

      GUILayout.EndScrollView();
    }
  }

  void refreshHostList()
  {
    // let the user know we are awaiting results from the master
      server
    loading = true;
    MasterServer.ClearHostList();
    MasterServer.RequestHostList( "GameTypeNameHere" );
  }

  // this is called when the Master Server reports an event to the
    client - for example, server registered successfully, host
    list received, etc
  void OnMasterServerEvent( MasterServerEvent msevent )
  {
    if( msevent == MasterServerEvent.HostListReceived )
    {
      // received the host list, no longer awaiting results
      loading = false;
    }
  }
}
```

The preceding code will list available servers registered to the Master Server. Clicking one of the buttons will call the Network.Connect function and connect to the corresponding server, and clicking on Refresh will display a **Loading...** message while results are fetched from the Master Server. There are a number of improvements and other tweaks that can be made to this code, left as an exercise for the reader:

- Refresh the host list every few seconds. This should be done transparently, without displaying a "Loading" message.

- Allow the user to add servers to a "favorites" list (possibly saved as CSV to PlayerPrefs), if your game allows players to run dedicated servers.

- If the user attempts to connect to a password-protected game (`HostData.passwordProtected` is true), display a password entry field.

- Save game information such as map, mode, and so on in the **Comments** field when registering a server, and allow the user to filter server results.

Setting up a dedicated server model

Many games allow players to host their own dedicated servers, as separate applications from the game client. Some games even allow players to modify the behavior of the server through scripting languages, allowing player-run servers to employ novel behaviors not originally designed into the game.

Let's see how we can set up a similar system in Unity. I will not be covering modding, although readers can look up Lua scripting in Unity—there are a number of resources on the topic.

Servers in Unity

Most games have a specialized "server" build, which contains much the same code as the client, designed to run as a dedicated server. This allows the server to process the same logic as the client.

Unity, however, does not directly support this concept out of the box. Unity Pro does allow builds to be run in "headless mode", which runs the game without initializing any graphics, resources, but the server runs the exact same code as the client. The game must be designed to operate in both server and client mode.

To do this, we'll take advantage of a compiler feature known as "conditional compilation". This allows us to wrap code in special tags which allows us to strip out entire sections of code when compiling. This way, our server-only code will only be included in server builds, and our client-only code will only be included in client builds.

Compiler directives

The first thing we will do, is figure out how the application knows whether it is a client or a server. We will use a compiler directive to do this.

If you are using Unity 4, you can go to **Edit | Project Settings | Player** and under **Other Settings** is a section that allows you to define these.

However, for any version prior to Unity 4, you'll have to define these yourself. To do this, create a new text file in the **Assets** folder and name it `smcs.rsp`. Open Notepad and type:

```
-define:SERVER
```

This creates a global symbol define for your C# scripts. You would use the symbol like this:

```
#if SERVER
    //code in here will not be compiled if SERVER isn't defined
#endif
```

You might consider writing an editor script which replaces the contents of this file (when compiling for the client, it would replace **SERVER** with **CLIENT**, and vice versa). It is important to note that changes to this file will not automatically recompile, when changing the file you should save one of your scripts. Your editor script might do this automatically, for example it could call `AssetDatabase.Refresh( ImportAssetOptions.ForceUpdate )`.

Now that we can detect whether the application was built as a server or a client, we'll need some way for the server to act as autonomously as possible. The server should have a configuration file which allows the user to set, for example, network settings before the server runs. This book will not cover how to load the configuration file (XML or JSON are recommended), but once these are loaded the server should immediately initialize and register itself with the Master Server using the data in the configuration file (for example, server name, maximum connections, listen port, password, and so on).

Setting up a server console without Pro

Usually, a game server is a console application. This is nearly possible in Unity if you have purchased a Pro license, by appending the `-batchmode` argument to the executable (actually, Unity does not create a console window, instead the game simply runs in the background). If you do have Pro, feel free to skip this section. However, if you own a free license, you'll need to get a bit creative.

We want the server to use as few resources as possible. We can create a script that turns off rendering of the scene when running in server mode. This won't completely disable the rendering system (as running in command line would), but it does significantly reduce the GPU load of the server.

```
using UnityEngine;
using System.Collections;

public class DisableServerCamera : MonoBehavior
```

```
{
#if SERVER
  void Update()
  {
    // culling mask is a bitmask - setting all bits to zero means
render nothing
    camera.cullingMask = 0;
  }
#endif
}
```

This script can be attached to a camera, and will cause that camera to not render anything when running on the server.

Next we're going to set up a console-type display for our server. This "console" will hook into the built-in Debug class and display a scrolling list of messages. We'll do this via Application.RegisterLogCallback.

```
using UnityEngine;
using System.Collections;
using System.Collections.Generic;

// contains data about the logged message
struct LogMessage
{
  public string message;
  public LogType type;
}

public class CustomLog : MonoBehavior
{
  // how many past log messages to store
  public int MaxHistory = 50;

  // a list of stored log messages
  private List<LogMessage> messages = new List<LogMessage>();

  // the position within the scroll view
  private Vector2 scrollPos = Vector2.zero;

  void OnEnable()
  {
    // register a custom log handler
    Application.RegisterLogCallback( HandleLog );
  }
```

```
  void OnDisable()
  {
    // unregister the log handler
    Application.RegisterLogCallback( null );
  }

  void OnGUI()
  {
    scrollPos = GUILayout.BeginScrollView( scrollPos, GUILayout.
ExpandWidth( true ), GUILayout.ExpandHeight( true ) );

    //draw each debug log - switch colors based on log type
    for( int i = 0; i < messages.Count; i++ )
    {
      Color color = Color.white;
      if( messages[i].type == LogType.Warning )
      {
        color = Color.yellow;
      }
      else if( messages[i].type != LogType.Log )
      {
        color = Color.red;
      }

      GUI.color = color;
      GUILayout.Label( messages[i].message );
    }

    GUILayout.EndScrollView();
  }

  void HandleLog( string message, string stackTrace, LogType type )
  {
    // add the message, remove entries if there's too many
    LogMessage msg = new LogMessage();
    msg.message = message;
    msg.type = type;

    messages.Add( msg );

    if( messages.Count >= MaxHistory )
    {
      messages.RemoveAt( 0 );
    }
```

```
        // scroll to the newest message by setting to a huge amount
        // will automatically be clamped
        scrollPos.y = 1000f;
    }
}
```

Now the user can see the debug information being printed as the server runs—very useful indeed.

You should strive for as much code reuse as possible in fact, if your game allows players to host a game from inside the client, most of the same code will already work with a few minor differences:

- As previously mentioned, the server starts up automatically with a configuration loaded from the user-editable files (unlike the client).
- The server does not spawn any player objects of its own, unlike the client.
- The server does not have any UIs or menus to display to the user beyond the log dump. Beyond starting up the server and shutting it down, there is zero interaction with the server application.

Loading networked levels

There are a few tricks to loading networked levels in the Unity game engine. If you just use `Application.LoadLevel`, you'll encounter a number of issues; specifically you may find that a client connecting to the game won't see any objects that were instantiated via `Network.Instantiate`. The reason for this is because the level loading process doesn't happen instantly—it actually takes two frames to complete. This occurs after the list of networked objects was received, so the load process will delete them.

Note that `Application.LoadLevel` is purely client side. Unity imposes no limitations on which level a client or server loads in a networked game. In fact, it's entirely possible that you might have different levels within a networked session, and this is what `Network.SetLevelPrefix` is for. Each of these levels is assigned some kind of "ID" that uniquely identifies the level. Before loading the level you would use `Network.SetLevelPrefix`. This essentially separates players into channels, so all players with level prefix 0 are separate from players with level prefix 1, for example.

Note that if your game needs all clients to load the same level, you'll have to ensure this yourself. If a client has a different level loaded than the host, without setting the level prefix to something different than the host, the client might see some odd situations, such as players floating or sunk into the ground (a player could be standing on a bridge in one level, and a different level at the same position might have a building; so the player would appear to be clipped into the building).

The correct way to load levels in a networked game, is to first disable the network queue, load the level, wait two frames, and then re-enable the network queue. This means any incoming messages will not be processed, and will instead be buffered until the new level has completely finished loading.

Let's write a simple network level loader that will handle all of these for us. It's designed as a singleton so we don't need one present in the scene (one will automatically be created):

```
using UnityEngine;
using System.Collections;

public class NetworkLevelLoader : MonoBehavior
  {
  // implements singleton-style behavior
  public static NetworkLevelLoader Instance
  {
    get
    {
      // no instance yet? Create a new one
      if( instance == null )
      {
        GameObject go = new GameObject( "_networkLevelLoader" );
        // hide it to avoid cluttering up the hieararchy
        go.hideFlags = HideFlags.HideInHierarchy;
        instance = go.AddComponent<NetworkLevelLoader>();

        // don't destroy it when a new scene loads
        GameObject.DontDestroyOnLoad( go );
      }
      return instance;
    }
  }
  private static NetworkLevelLoader instance;

  public void LoadLevel( string levelName, int prefix = 0 )
  {
    StopAllCoroutines();
```

```
          StartCoroutine( doLoadLevel( levelName, prefix ) );
       }

       // do the work of pausing the network queue, loading the level,
          waiting, and then unpausing
       IEnumerator doLoadLevel( string name, int prefix )
       {
          Network.SetSendingEnabled( 0, false );
          Network.isMessageQueueRunning = false;

          Network.SetLevelPrefix( prefix );
          Application.LoadLevel( name );
          yield return null;
          yield return null;

          Network.isMessageQueueRunning = true;
          Network.SetSendingEnabled( 0, true );
       }
   }
```

You can now replace any calls to Application.LoadLevel with
NetworkLevelLoader.Instance.LoadLevel. For example, the server might call an
RPC which loads the level via the helper class we just wrote, as a buffered RPC so
that all clients connecting will automatically load the level.

> If your server needs to change level during the connection, for example,
> in many FPS games players can vote on a new map at the end of a
> round, things get a bit more complicated. The server should first delete
> all networked objects belonging to players, remove RPCs from all
> players (via Network.RemoveRPCs), and then call the load-level RPC.

Creating a multiplayer Pong game

Now that we've covered the basics of using Unity Networking, we're going to apply
them to creating a multiplayer Pong clone.

The game will play pretty much as standard Pong. Players can choose their name,
and then view a list of open servers (full rooms will not be shown). Players can also
host their own game.

Once in a game, players bounce a ball back and forth until it hits the opponent's side. Players get one point for this, and the ball will reset and continue bouncing. When a player hits 10 points, the winner is called, the scores are reset, and the game continues. While in a match with no other players, the server will inform the user to wait. If a player leaves, the match is reset (if the host leaves, the other player is automatically disconnected).

Preparing the Field

First, create a cube (by navigating to **GameObject | Create Other | Cube**) and scale it to 1 x 1 x 4. Name it Paddle and set the **Tag** to **Player**. Check the **Is Trigger** box on the collider.

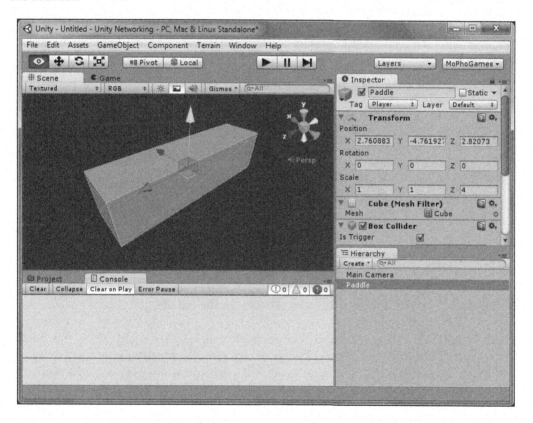

Our ball will detect when it hits the trigger zone on the player paddle, and reverse direction. We use triggers because we don't necessarily want to simulate the ball realistically with the Unity physics engine (we get far less control over the ball's physics, and it may not behave exactly as we would like).

We will also line our playing field in trigger boxes. For these you can duplicate the paddle four times and form a large rectangle outlining the playing field. The actual size doesn't matter so much, as long as the ball has room to move around. We will add two more tags for these boundaries: **Boundary** and **Goal**. The two boxes on the top and bottom of the field are tagged as **Boundary**, the two boxes on the left and right are tagged as **Goal**.

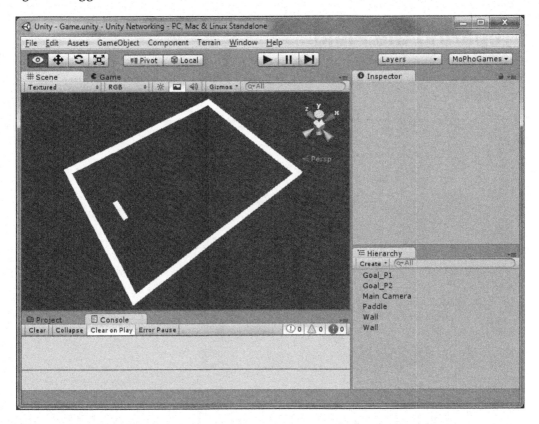

When the ball hits a trigger tagged Boundary, it reverses its velocity along the z axis. When the ball hits a trigger tagged Player, it reverses its velocity along the x axis. And when a ball hits a trigger tagged Goal, the corresponding player gets a point and the ball resets.

Let's finish up the playing field before writing our code:

1. Firstly, set the camera to **Orthographic** and position it at (0, 10, 0). Rotate it 90 degrees along the x axis until it points straight down, and change its **Orthographic Size** to a value large enough to frame the playing field (in my case, I set it to 15). Set the camera's background color to black.

2. Create a directional light that points straight down. This will illuminate the paddles and ball to make them pure white.

3. Finally, duplicate the player paddle and move it to the other half of the field.

The Ball script

Now we're going to create the Ball script. We'll add the multiplayer code later, for now this is offline only:

```
using UnityEngine;
using System.Collections;

public class Ball : MonoBehavior
{
  // the speed the ball starts with
  public float StartSpeed = 5f;

  // the maximum speed of the ball
  public float MaxSpeed = 20f;

  // how much faster the ball gets with each bounce
  public float SpeedIncrease = 0.25f;

  // the current speed of the ball
  private float currentSpeed;

  // the current direction of travel
  private Vector2 currentDir;

  // whether or not the ball is resetting
  private bool resetting = false;

  void Start()
  {
    // initialize starting speed
    currentSpeed = StartSpeed;

    // initialize direction
    currentDir = Random.insideUnitCircle.normalized;
  }

  void Update()
  {
    // don't move the ball if it's resetting
```

```
    if( resetting )
      return;

    // move the ball in the current direction
    Vector2 moveDir = currentDir * currentSpeed * Time.deltaTime;
    transform.Translate( new Vector3( moveDir.x, 0f, moveDir.y ) );
}

void OnTriggerEnter( Collider other )
{
  if( other.tag == "Boundary" )
  {
    // vertical boundary, reverse Y direction
    currentDir.y *= -1;
  }
  else if( other.tag == "Player" )
  {
    // player paddle, reverse X direction
    currentDir.x *= -1;
  }
  else if( other.tag == "Goal" )
  {
    // reset the ball
    StartCoroutine( resetBall() );
    // inform goal of the score
    other.SendMessage( "GetPoint",
      SendMessageOptions.DontRequireReceiver );
  }

  // increase speed
  currentSpeed += SpeedIncrease;

  // clamp speed to maximum
  currentSpeed = Mathf.Clamp( currentSpeed, StartSpeed, MaxSpeed );
}

IEnumerator resetBall()
{
  // reset position, speed, and direction
  resetting = true;
  transform.position = Vector3.zero;

  currentDir = Vector3.zero;
  currentSpeed = 0f;
```

```
    // wait for 3 seconds before starting the round
    yield return new WaitForSeconds( 3f );

Start();

    resetting = false;
  }
}
```

To create the ball, as before we'll create a cube. It will have the default scale of 1 x 1 x 1. Set the position to origin (0, 0, 0). Add a rigidbody component to the cube, untick the **Use Gravity** checkbox, and tick the **Is Kinematic** checkbox. The Rigidbody component is used to let our ball get the OnTriggerEnter events. **Is Kinematic** is enabled because we're controlling the ball ourselves, rather than using Unity's physics engine.

Add the new **Ball** component that we just created and test the game. It should look something like this:

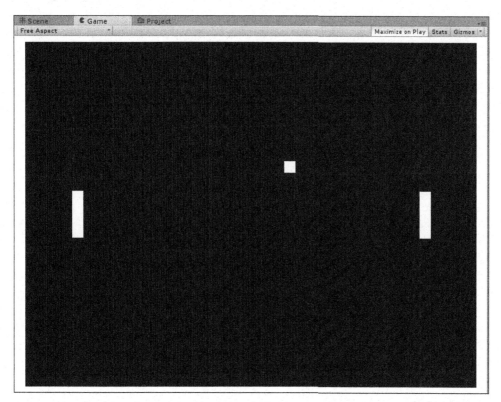

You should see the ball bouncing around the field. If it hits either side, it will move back to the center of the field, pause for 3 seconds, and then begin moving again. This should happen fairly quickly, because the paddles aren't usable yet (the ball will often bounce right past them).

The Paddle script

Let's add player control to the mix. Note that at the moment player paddles will both move in tandem, with the same controls. This is OK, later we'll disable the player input based on whether or not the network view belongs to the local client (this is what the AcceptsInput field is for):

```
using UnityEngine;
using System.Collections;

public class Paddle : MonoBehavior
{
  // how fast the paddle can move
  public float MoveSpeed = 10f;

  // how far up and down the paddle can move
  public float MoveRange = 10f;

  // whether this paddle can accept player input
  public bool AcceptsInput = true;

  void Update()
  {
    // does not accept input, abort
    if( !AcceptsInput )
      return;

    //get user input
    float input = Input.GetAxis( "Vertical" );

    // move paddle
    Vector3 pos = transform.position;
    pos.z += input * MoveSpeed * Time.deltaTime;
    // clamp paddle position
    pos.z = Mathf.Clamp( pos.z, -MoveRange, MoveRange );
    // set position
    transform.position = pos;
  }
}
```

You can now move the paddles up and down, and bounce the ball back and forth. The ball will slowly pick up speed as it bounces, until it hits either of the goals. When that happens, the round resets.

Keeping score

What we're going to do now is create a scorekeeper. The scorekeeper will keep track of both players' scores, and will later keep track of other things, such as whether we're waiting for another player to join:

```
using UnityEngine;
using System.Collections;

public class Scorekeeper : MonoBehavior
{
  // the maximum score a player can reach
  public int ScoreLimit = 10;

  // Player 1's score
  private int p1Score = 0;

  // Player 2's score
  private int p2Score = 0;

  // give the appropriate player a point
  public void AddScore( int player )
  {
    // player 1
    if( player == 1 )
    {
      p1Score++;
    }
    // player 2
    else if( player == 2 )
    {
      p2Score++;
    }

    // check if either player reached the score limit
    if( p1Score >= ScoreLimit || p2Score >= ScoreLimit )
    {
      // player 1 has a better score than player 2
      if( p1score > p2score )
        Debug.Log( "Player 1 wins" );
```

```
        // player 2 has a better score than player 1
        if( p2score > p1score )
          Debug.Log( "Player 2 wins" );
        // both players have the same score - tie
        else
          Debug.Log( "Players are tied" );

        // reset scores and start over
        p1Score = 0;
        p2Score = 0;
      }
    }
  }
}
```

Now our scorekeeper can keep score for each player, let's make the goals and add points with a Goal script. It's a very simple script, which reacts to the GetPoint message sent from the ball upon collision to give the other player a point:

```
using UnityEngine;
using System.Collections;

public class Goal : MonoBehavior
{
  // the player who gets a point for this goal, 1 or 2
  public int Player = 1;

  // the Scorekeeper
  public Scorekeeper scorekeeper;

  public void GetPoint()
  {
    // when the ball collides with this goal, give the player a point
    scorekeeper.AddScore( Player );
  }
}
```

Attach this script to both goals. For player 1's goal, set the **Player** to 2 (player 2 gets a point when the ball lands in player 1's goal), for player 2's goal, set the **Player** to 1 (player 1 gets a point when the ball lands in player 2's goal).

The game is almost completely functional now (aside from multiplayer). One problem is that we can't tell that points are being given until the game ends, so let's add a score display.

Displaying the score to the player

Create two 3D Text objects as children of the scorekeeper. Name them p1Score and P2Score, and position them on each side of the field:

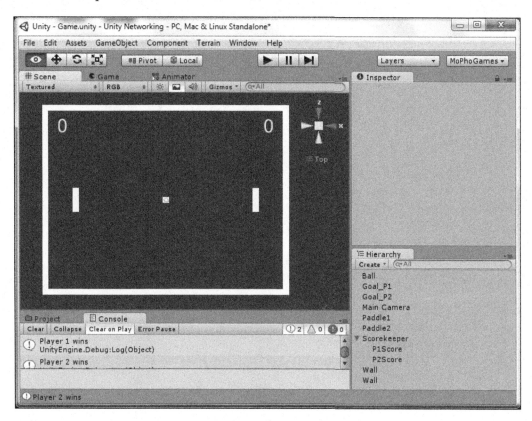

Let's make the scorekeeper display the player scores:

```
using UnityEngine;
using System.Collections;

public class Scorekeeper : MonoBehavior
{
  // the maximum score a player can reach
  public int ScoreLimit = 10;

  // the display test for player 1's score
  public TextMesh Player1ScoreDisplay;

  // the display text for player 2's score
```

```
    public TextMesh Player2ScoreDisplay;
// Player 1's score
private int p1Score = 0;

// Player 2's score
private int p2Score = 0;

// give the appropriate player a point
public void AddScore( int player )
{
  // player 1
  if( player == 1 )
  {
    p1Score++;
  }
  // player 2
  else if( player == 2 )
  {
    p2Score++;
  }
  // check if either player reached the score limit
  if( p1Score >= ScoreLimit || p2Score >= ScoreLimit )
  {
    // player 1 has a better score than player 2
    if( p1Score > p2Score )
      Debug.Log( "Player 1 wins" );
    // player 2 has a better score than player 1
    if( p2Score > p1Score )
      Debug.Log( "Player 2 wins" );
    // both players have the same score - tie
    else
      Debug.Log( "Players are tied" );

    // reset scores and start over
    p1Score = 0;
    p2Score = 0;
  }

  // display each player's score
  Player1ScoreDisplay.text = p1Score.ToString();
  Player2ScoreDisplay.text = p2Score.ToString();
  }
}
```

The score is now displayed properly when a player gets a point. Be sure to give it a test run—the ball should bounce around the field, and you should be able to deflect the ball with the paddle. If the ball hits player 1's goal, player 2 should get 1 point, and vice versa. If one player gets 10 points, both scores should reset to zero, the ball should move back to the center of the screen, and the game should restart.

With the most important gameplay elements complete, we can start working on multiplayer networking.

Networking the game

For testing purposes, let's launch a network game as soon as the level is launched:

```
using UnityEngine;
using System.Collections;

public class RequireNetwork : MonoBehavior
{
  void Awake()
  {
    if( Network.peerType == NetworkPeerType.Disconnected )
      Network.InitializeServer( 1, 25005, true );
  }
}
```

If we start this level without hosting a server first, it will automatically do so for us in ensuring that the networked code still works.

Now we can start converting our code to work in multiplayer.

Let's start by networking the paddle code:

```
using UnityEngine;
using System.Collections;

public class Paddle : MonoBehavior
{
  // how fast the paddle can move
  public float MoveSpeed = 10f;

  // how far up and down the paddle can move
  public float MoveRange = 10f;

  // whether this paddle can accept player input
  public bool AcceptsInput = true;
```

```csharp
// the position read from the network
// used for interpolation
private Vector3 readNetworkPos;

void Start()
{
  // if this is our paddle, it accepts input
  // otherwise, if it is someone else's paddle, it does not
  AcceptsInput = networkView.isMine;
}

void Update()
{
  // does not accept input, interpolate network pos
  if( !AcceptsInput )
  {
    transform.position = Vector3.Lerp( transform.position,
      readNetworkPos, 10f * Time.deltaTime );

    // don't use player input
    return;
  }

  //get user input
  float input = Input.GetAxis( "Vertical" );

  // move paddle
  Vector3 pos = transform.position;
  pos.z += input * MoveSpeed * Time.deltaTime;

  // clamp paddle position
  pos.z = Mathf.Clamp( pos.z, -MoveRange, MoveRange );

  // set position
  transform.position = pos;
}

void OnSerializeNetworkView( BitStream stream )
{
  // writing information, push current paddle position
  if( stream.isWriting )
  {
    Vector3 pos = transform.position;
    stream.Serialize( ref pos );
```

```
    }
    // reading information, read paddle position
    else
    {
      Vector3 pos = Vector3.zero;
      stream.Serialize( ref pos );
      readNetworkPos = pos;
    }
  }
}
```

The paddle will detect whether it is owned by the local player or not. If not, it will not accept player input, instead it will interpolate its position to the last read position value over the network.

By default, network views will serialize the attached transform. This is OK for testing, but should not be used for production. Without any interpolation, the movement will appear very laggy and jerky, as positions are sent a fixed number of times per second (15 by default in Unity Networking) in order to save on bandwidth, so snapping to the position 15 times per second will look jerky. In order to solve this, rather than instantly snapping to the new position we smoothly interpolate towards it. In this case, we use the frame delta multiplied by a number (larger is faster, smaller is slower), which produces an easing motion; the object starts quickly approaching the target value, slowing down as it gets closer.

When serializing, it either reads the position and stores it, or it sends the current transform position, depending on whether the stream is for reading or for writing.

Now, add a **Network View** to one of your paddles, drag the panel component attached to the **Paddle** into the **Observed** slot, and make it a prefab by dragging it into your **Project** pane.

Next, delete the paddles in the scene, and create two empty game objects where the paddles used to be positioned. These will be the starting points for each paddle when spawned.

Spawning paddles

Next, let's make the scorekeeper spawn these paddles. The scorekeeper, upon a player connecting, will send an RPC to them to spawn a paddle:

```
using UnityEngine;
using System.Collections;

public class Scorekeeper : MonoBehavior
```

```
{
    // the maximum score a player can reach
    public int ScoreLimit = 10;

    // the start points for each player paddle
    public Transform SpawnP1;
    public Transform SpawnP2;

    // the paddle prefab
    public GameObject paddlePrefab;

    // the display test for player 1's score
    public TextMesh Player1ScoreDisplay;

    // the display text for player 2's score
    public TextMesh Player2ScoreDisplay;

    // Player 1's score
    private int p1Score = 0;

    // Player 2's score
    private int p2Score = 0;

    void Start()
    {
        if( Network.isServer )
        {
            // server doesn't trigger OnPlayerConnected, manually spawn
            Network.Instantiate( paddlePrefab, SpawnP1.position,
                Quaternion.identity, 0 );
        }
    }

void OnPlayerConnected( NetworkPlayer player )
    {
        // when a player joins, tell them to spawn
        networkView.RPC( "net_DoSpawn", player, SpawnP2.position );
    }

    [RPC]
    void net_DoSpawn( Vector3 position )
    {
        // spawn the player paddle
```

```
    Network.Instantiate( paddlePrefab, position,
      Quaternion.identity, 0 );
  }

  // give the appropriate player a point
  public void AddScore( int player )
  {
    // player 1
    if( player == 1 )
    {
      p1Score++;
    }
    // player 2
    else if( player == 2 )
    {
      p2Score++;
    }

    // check if either player reached the score limit
    if( p1Score >= ScoreLimit || p2Score >= ScoreLimit )
    {
      // player 1 has a better score than player 2
      if( p1Score > p2Score )
        Debug.Log( "Player 1 wins" );
      // player 2 has a better score than player 1
      if( p2Score > p1Score )
        Debug.Log( "Player 2 wins" );
      // both players have the same score - tie
      else
        Debug.Log( "Players are tied" );

      // reset scores and start over
      p1Score = 0;
      p2Score = 0;
    }

    // display each player's score
    Player1ScoreDisplay.text = p1Score.ToString();
    Player2ScoreDisplay.text = p2Score.ToString();
  }
}
```

At the moment, when you start the game, one paddle spawns for player 1, but player 2 is missing (there's nobody else playing). However, the ball eventually flies off toward player 2's side, and gives player 1 a free point.

The networked ball

Let's keep the ball frozen in place when there's nobody to play against, or if we aren't the server. We're also going to add networked movement to our ball:

```
using UnityEngine;
using System.Collections;

public class Ball : MonoBehavior
{
  // the speed the ball starts with
  public float StartSpeed = 5f;

  // the maximum speed of the ball
  public float MaxSpeed = 20f;

  // how much faster the ball gets with each bounce
  public float SpeedIncrease = 0.25f;

  // the current speed of the ball
  private float currentSpeed;

  // the current direction of travel
  private Vector2 currentDir;

  // whether or not the ball is resetting
  private bool resetting = false;

  void Start()
  {
    // initialize starting speed
    currentSpeed = StartSpeed;

    // initialize direction
    currentDir = Random.insideUnitCircle.normalized;
  }

  void Update()
  {
    // don't move the ball if it's resetting
```

```
    if( resetting )
      return;

    // don't move the ball if there's nobody to play with
    if( Network.connections.Length == 0 )
      return;

    // move the ball in the current direction
    Vector2 moveDir = currentDir * currentSpeed * Time.deltaTime;
    transform.Translate( new Vector3( moveDir.x, 0f, moveDir.y ) );
  }


  void OnTriggerEnter( Collider other )
  {
    // bounce off the top and bottom walls
    if( other.tag == "Boundary" )
    {
      // vertical boundary, reverse Y direction
      currentDir.y *= -1;
    }
    // bounce off the player paddle
    else if( other.tag == "Player" )
    {
      // player paddle, reverse X direction
      currentDir.x *= -1;
    }
    // if we hit a goal, and we are the server, give the
       appropriate player a point
    else if( other.tag == "Goal" && Network.isServer )
    {
      // reset the ball
      StartCoroutine( resetBall() );
      // inform goal of the score
      other.SendMessage( "GetPoint", SendMessageOptions.
        DontRequireReceiver );
    }

    // increase speed
    currentSpeed += SpeedIncrease;

    // clamp speed to maximum
    currentSpeed = Mathf.Clamp( currentSpeed, StartSpeed, MaxSpeed );
  }
```

```
IEnumerator resetBall()
{
  // reset position, speed, and direction
  resetting = true;
  transform.position = Vector3.zero;

  currentDir = Vector3.zero;
  currentSpeed = 0f;

  // wait for 3 seconds before starting the round
  yield return new WaitForSeconds( 3f );

  Start();

  resetting = false;
}

void OnSerializeNetworkView( BitStream stream )
{
  //write position, direction, and speed to network
  if( stream.isWriting )
  {
    Vector3 pos = transform.position;
    Vector3 dir = currentDir;
    float speed = currentSpeed;
    stream.Serialize( ref pos );
    stream.Serialize( ref dir );
    stream.Serialize( ref speed );
  }
  // read position, direction, and speed from network
  else
  {
    Vector3 pos = Vector3.zero;
    Vector3 dir = Vector3.zero;
    float speed = 0f;
    stream.Serialize( ref pos );
    stream.Serialize( ref dir );
    stream.Serialize( ref speed );
    transform.position = pos;
    currentDir = dir;
    currentSpeed = speed;
  }
}
}
```

The ball will stay put if there's nobody to play against, and if someone we're playing against leaves, the ball will reset to the middle of the field. The ball will also work correctly on multiple machines at once (it is simulated on the server, and position/ velocity is relayed to clients). Add NetworkView to the ball and have it observe the Ball component.

Networked scorekeeping

There is one final piece of the puzzle that is keeping score. We're going to convert our AddScore function to use an RPC, and if a player leaves we will also reset the scores:

```
using UnityEngine;
using System.Collections;

public class Scorekeeper : MonoBehavior
{
  // the maximum score a player can reach
  public int ScoreLimit = 10;

  // the start points for each player paddle
  public Transform SpawnP1;
  public Transform SpawnP2;

  // the paddle prefab
  public GameObject paddlePrefab;

  // the display test for player 1's score
  public TextMesh Player1ScoreDisplay;

  // the display text for player 2's score
  public TextMesh Player2ScoreDisplay;

  // Player 1's score
  private int p1Score = 0;

  // Player 2's score
  private int p2Score = 0;

  void Start()
  {
    if( Network.isServer )
    {
```

```
        // server doesn't trigger OnPlayerConnected, manually spawn
        Network.Instantiate( paddlePrefab, SpawnP1.position,
          Quaternion.identity, 0 );

        // nobody has joined yet, display "Waiting..." for player 2
        Player2ScoreDisplay.text = "Waiting...";
    }
}

void OnPlayerConnected( NetworkPlayer player )
{
    // when a player joins, tell them to spawn
    networkView.RPC( "net_DoSpawn", player, SpawnP2.position );

    // change player 2's score display from "waiting..." to "0"
    Player2ScoreDisplay.text = "0";
}

void OnPlayerDisconnected( NetworkPlayer player )
{
    // player 2 left, reset scores
    p1Score = 0;
    p2Score = 0;

    // display each player's scores
    // display "Waiting..." for player 2
    Player1ScoreDisplay.text = p1Score.ToString();
    Player2ScoreDisplay.text = "Waiting...";
}

void OnDisconnectedFromServer( NetworkDisconnection cause )
{
    // go back to the main menu
    Application.LoadLevel( "Menu" );
}

[RPC]
void net_DoSpawn( Vector3 position )
{
    // spawn the player paddle
    Network.Instantiate( paddlePrefab, position,
      Quaternion.identity, 0 );
}
```

```csharp
// call an RPC to give the player a point
public void AddScore( int player )
{
  networkView.RPC( "net_AddScore", RPCMode.All, player );
}


// give the appropriate player a point
[RPC]
public void net_AddScore( int player )
{
  // player 1
  if( player == 1 )
  {
    p1Score++;
  }
  // player 2
  else if( player == 2 )
  {
    p2Score++;
  }

  // check if either player reached the score limit
  if( p1Score >= ScoreLimit || p2Score >= ScoreLimit )
  {
    // player 1 has a better score than player 2
    if( p1Score > p2Score )
      Debug.Log( "Player 1 wins" );
    // player 2 has a better score than player 1
    if( p2Score > p1Score )
      Debug.Log( "Player 2 wins" );
    // both players have the same score - tie
    else
      Debug.Log( "Players are tied" );

    // reset scores and start over
    p1Score = 0;
    p2Score = 0;
  }

  // display each player's score
  Player1ScoreDisplay.text = p1Score.ToString();
  Player2ScoreDisplay.text = p2Score.ToString();
}
}
```

Our game is fully networked at this point. The only problem is that we do not yet have a way to connect to the game. Let's write a simple direct connect dialog which allows players to enter an IP address to join.

 With direct IP connect, note that NAT punch-through is not possible. When you use the Master Server, you can pass either HostData or GUID of a host which will perform NAT punch-through.

The Connect screen

The following script shows the player IP and Port entry fields, and the **Connect** and **Host** buttons. The player can directly connect to an IP and Port, or start a server on the given Port. By using direct connect we don't need to rely on a master server, as players directly connect to games via IP. If you wanted to, you could easily create a lobby screen for this instead of using direct connect (allowing players to browse a list of running servers instead of manually typing IP address). To keep things simpler, we'll omit the lobby screen in this example:

```
using UnityEngine;
using System.Collections;

public class ConnectToGame : MonoBehavior
{
  private string ip = "";
  private int port = 25005;

  void OnGUI()
  {
    // let the user enter IP address
    GUILayout.Label( "IP Address" );
    ip = GUILayout.TextField( ip, GUILayout.Width( 200f ) );

    // let the user enter port number
    // port is an integer, so only numbers are allowed
    GUILayout.Label( "Port" );
    string port_str = GUILayout.TextField( port.ToString(),
      GUILayout.Width( 100f ) );
    int port_num = port;
    if( int.TryParse( port_str, out port_num ) )
      port = port_num;
```

```
  // connect to the IP and port
  if( GUILayout.Button( "Connect", GUILayout.Width( 100f ) ) )
  {
    Network.Connect( ip, port );
  }

  // host a server on the given port, only allow 1 incoming
      connection (one other player)
  if( GUILayout.Button( "Host", GUILayout.Width( 100f ) ) )
  {
    Network.InitializeServer( 1, port, true );
  }
}

void OnConnectedToServer()
{
  Debug.Log( "Connected to server" );
  // this is the NetworkLevelLoader we wrote earlier in the
      chapter - pauses the network, loads the level, waits for the
      level to finish, and then unpauses the network
  NetworkLevelLoader.Instance.LoadLevel( "Game" );
}

void OnServerInitialized()
{
  Debug.Log( "Server initialized" );
  NetworkLevelLoader.Instance.LoadLevel( "Game" );
}
}
```

With this, we now have a complete, fully functional multiplayer Pong game. Players can host games, as well as join them if they know the IP.

When in a game as the host, the game will wait for another player to show up before starting the game. If the other player leaves, the game will reset and wait again. As a player, if the host leaves it goes back to the main menu.

Summary

In this chapter, we covered:

- The basics of UDP and reliable/unreliable communication
- Setting up a lobby server
- What a Network View is
- How to serialize object state
- How to send reliable RPCs
- Hosting game servers and connecting to them
- Registering servers with the lobby
- The basics of dedicated servers
- How to load levels in a networked game

We applied these concepts to create a multiplayer clone of Pong in Unity.

In the next chapter, we will cover a third-party alternative to Unity Networking, known as Photon Unity Networking.

2
Photon Unity Networking – The Chat Client

In the last chapter, we reviewed the Unity Networking API provided with the Unity game engine. In this chapter, we will review an alternative to Unity Networking, called **Photon Unity Networking (PUN)**.

In this chapter, we will cover:

- How PUN works
- The differences and similarities between PUN and Unity Networking
- Setting up PUN with Photon Cloud
- Using PhotonViews
- Connecting to Photon
- Getting a list of rooms
- Creating and joining rooms
- Filtering lobby results by preference
- Automatic matchmaking
- Using FindFriends
- Syncing a level between players
- At the end of the chapter, we will create a chat client built on top of PUN

Photon Unity Networking is provided by ExitGames. It aims to provide an API consistent with Unity Networking, while at the same time solving many of the issues with Unity Networking, such as the dreaded NAT punch-through problem (players behind NAT are often unable to host games).

Photon Unity Networking works with another service known as **Photon Cloud**. Just like Unity Networking, Photon Unity Networking uses UDP for communication, but the key difference is that players don't directly host servers. Instead, clients connect to a server cluster (known as the "cloud") and request a room. A room will be created on one of the servers in the cluster, and clients connect to this room.

This, in almost all cases, solves the aforementioned NAT issues with Unity, as all the players connect to a public server (with the ideal network configuration) instead of connecting directly to each other. Rather than making players do port-forwarding and other workarounds to get their private, self-hosted server visible to the public, servers are hosted externally and all of the work is done already. Players don't connect to each other anymore, they simply connect to a server which acts as a middleman for communication.

Additionally, rather than having a "host" (which would normally be the player who hosts the server), Photon Unity Networking defines a "master client". The player to create a room is, by default, the master client. However, if that player leaves, another player will be chosen to be the master client. Contrast this to Unity Networking, where if a host leaves, the game is simply ended or must be migrated, in PUN the game can seamlessly continue.

Differences between PUN and Unity Networking

PUN provides a consistent, familiar API to those who have already worked with Unity Networking. However, there are many key differences and some code is not compatible without changes.

In PUN, nearly all of the main functions are contained in the `PhotonNetwork` class (meant to be analogous to the `Network` class in Unity). There is no MasterServer equivalent in PUN: all the required functions are moved to the `PhotonNetwork` class.

Rather than initializing servers, in PUN you create "rooms" via `PhotonNetwork.CreateRoom`. Rooms are essentially partitions on the game server to separate groups of players from each other.

There is no longer a concept of host IP. Instead, to connect to a room, you pass either `Room` to the `JoinRoom` function, or you pass the name of the room (room names are required to be unique).

Because of the way Photon Unity Networking works, direct LAN connection is not possible as rather than connecting to each other, players connect to a central server cluster. Players are required to be connected to the Internet to play with each other, even if they are on the same local network.

PUN also has PhotonViews, rather than NetworkViews, although they serve a very similar purpose. State serialization is done via the `OnSerializePhotonView` method, and RPC calls work almost exactly the same way they do in Unity.

 There is a key difference in behavior between the **PUN RPC** calls and **Unity RPC** calls. In Unity, unless you broadcast a message to all, you can't directly send a message to yourself. However, PUN does not have this restriction.

There is one very big difference between Photon Unity Networking and Unity Networking. Whereas `Network.Instantiate` simply takes a prefab and instantiates it, `PhotonNetwork.Instantiate` does not have access to many of the things `Network.Instantiate` makes use of (for example, `Network.Instantiate` likely sends some kind of metadata like an asset ID which can be used to instantiate the object on the receiving end). So `PhotonNetwork.Instantiate` instead takes a string for the name of the object, and it will load the object from a `Resources` folder in your project (via `Resources.Load`). Therefore, all of your networked objects need to be included in a `Resources` folder.

Now that we've covered what makes PUN different, let's get started setting up PUN and Photon Cloud

Setting up PUN with Photon Cloud

To begin, go ahead and sign up for Photon Cloud at:

`https://cloud.exitgames.com`

After you've created an account, go to the Dashboard (**My Photon | Applications**) and create a new Application. The name is not important, but you'll want to copy the ID for later.

Next, visit the **Asset Store** and search for **Photon Unity Networking**. The first asset you see should be **Photon Unity Networking Free**. Download this asset into your project.

Upon downloading the plugin, and importing via **Assets | Import Package | Custom Package**, you are prompted with a window asking you to sign up, enter an app ID, or setup a custom-hosted server.

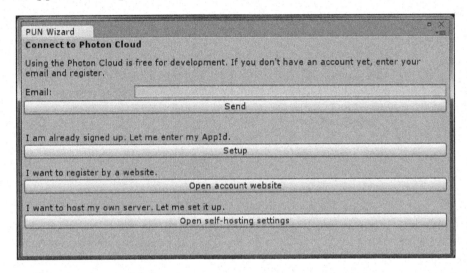

Click on the **Setup** option, assuming you have already created an account with Photon Cloud. Select which region you want to use by default, and paste the ID you copied from the website into the **AppId** field, and click on **Save**.

You are now ready to begin using the PUN plugin.

 Photon relies on sockets to connect, and while it does work in webplayer or standalone builds with Unity Free, it does not work on iOS or Android builds with the free license (since these disallow use of .NET sockets). However, in some cases there appears to be undocumented Android support on the 30 day Pro trial.

Using PhotonViews

Photon Unity Networking features PhotonViews. These essentially act exactly as their Unity Networking counterpart, allowing an object to serialize its state and send RPCs over the network. Nearly every part of PhotonView is equivalent to Network View, with a few script differences.

If you want to get the PhotonView for an object, you have two options: you can either call the static `PhotonView.Get` method, use `GetComponent<PhotonView>()`, or you can have your script inherit from `Photon.MonoBehaviour` and use `this.photonView` to get the view.

To serialize object state, add the `OnPhotonSerializeView` function to your script. This function takes a PhotonStream, and a PhotonMessageInfo. This works exactly like serialization in Unity Networking.

To call RPCs, you can call the RPC function on the PhotonView. As with Unity Networking, RPC methods are marked with the `[RPC]` attribute.

Here's an example that serializes position and calls an RPC when the spacebar is pressed:

```
using UnityEngine;
using System.Collections;

public class Example_PhotonView : Photon.MonoBehaviour
{
  void Update()
  {
    if( photonView.isMine )
    {
      // if the space key is pressed, and this photon view belongs
         to the local player, call the RPC
      if( Input.GetKeyDown( KeyCode.Space ) )
      {
        photonView.RPC( "TestRPC", PhotonTargets.All );
      }
    }
  }
}
```

```
[RPC]
void TestRPC()
{
  Debug.Log( "An RPC was called!" );
}


void OnPhotonSerializeView( PhotonStream stream,
  PhotonMessageInfo info )
{
  if( stream.isWriting )
  {
    // writing to the stream, send position
    stream.SendNext( transform.position );
  }
  else
  {
    // reading from the stream, get position
    transform.position = (Vector3)stream.ReceiveNext();
  }
}
}
```

Note the minor API changes between Photon and Unity. The two are not always completely compatible, but there is almost always an equivalent function call from one to the other.

Connecting to Photon and getting a list of rooms

Let's connect to Photon Cloud. There are three main ways of doing this:

- You can call `PhotonNetwork.ConnectUsingSettings` which will connect via the settings defined in the editor panel
- You can call `PhotonNetwork.ConnectToBestCloudServer` which will ping each available server cluster and connect to the best one
- You can call `PhotonNetwork.Connect`, passing the server address of the appropriate Photon region and the port
- You can also use `ConnectUsingSettings` which will connect to the region we defined in the editor panel. We'll be using this for the rest of the chapter

If you wish to use **Connect manually**, as of the time of writing, the addresses for each region are:

US (East Coast): app-us.exitgamescloud.com

EU (Amsterdam): app-eu.exitgamescloud.com

Asia (Singapore): app-asia.exitgamescloud.com

Japan (Tokyo): app-jp.exitgamescloud.com

And the port to connect on can be read from the static ServerSettings.DefaultMasterPort field. You will also have to provide your app ID to the connect function.

For instance, a script to connect to Photon and display a list of rooms currently open is as follows:

```
using UnityEngine;
using System.Collections;

public class Example_ConnectToPhoton : MonoBehaviour
{
  bool joined = false;

  void Start()
  {
    // connect to Photon
    PhotonNetwork.ConnectUsingSettings( "v1.0" );
  }

  void OnJoinedLobby()
  {
    // we joined Photon and are ready to get a list of rooms
    joined = true;
  }

  void OnFailedToConnectToPhoton( DisconnectCause cause )
  {
    // some error occurred, 'cause' is an enumeration of the
      error that happened
  }
```

```
        void OnGUI()
        {
          if( !joined && string.IsNullOrEmpty( error ) )
          {
            // we're still connecting to photon, display a loading GUI
          }
          else if( joined )
          {
            // we're connected to Photon, so now we can draw the
              lobby screen

            drawLobby();
          }
        }


        void drawLobby()
        {
          // no rooms available
          if( PhotonNetwork.GetRoomList().Length == 0 )
          {
            // display a message informing the user that there aren't
              any rooms available to join
          }
          // draw each room in a scroll view
          else
          {
            foreach( RoomInfo room in PhotonNetwork.GetRoomList() )
            {
              // draw the room info to the GUI
            }

          }
        }
      }
```

Notice that we only use `GetRoomList`, unlike in Unity Networking where we would use `GetHostList` and `PollHostList`. In Photon, this room list is automatically updated in near real time, so there's no need to manually download the list from the server. If you need some kind of Refresh functionality, you can simply grab the results from GetRoomList and cache the results.

Creating and joining rooms

Let us have a look at how to create rooms.

Creating rooms

To create a room in PUN, use the `CreateRoom` function:

```
using UnityEngine;
using System.Collections;

public class Example_CreateRoom : MonoBehaviour
{
  void OnGUI()
  {
    // if we're not inside a room, let the player create a room
    if( PhotonNetwork.room == null )
    {

      // if create room button clicked
      {
        // create a room called "RoomNameHere", visible to the
          lobby, allows other players to join, and allows up to 8
          players
        PhotonNetwork.CreateRoom( "RoomNameHere", true, true, 8 );
      }
    }
    else
    {
      // we're connected to a room, display some info such as room
        name, player count, etc.

      // disconnect from the current room
      // if disconnect button clicked
      {
        PhotonNetwork.LeaveRoom();
      }
    }
  }
}
```

Creating a room triggers the following callbacks:

- `OnCreatedRoom`, if the room is successfully created.

- `OnPhotonCreateRoomFailed`, if the call to CreateRoom failed. Unfortunately, no parameters are sent, so it's impossible to truly know the reason (however, the most likely reason is that the room name is already in use).

- Note that there is no naming convention for rooms, but room names must be unique (otherwise the room creation will fail). Uniqueness is enforced on a per-app basis. You can also provide `null` to have a unique room name generated for you.

You can also specify a maximum number of players for the room. Unlike Unity Networking, this is exactly the number of players which can play, including the host (whereas in Unity networking, this number does not include the host, so specifying 8 players allows 9 players to play if the host participates).

Photon Cloud will automatically close rooms if all players leave the game.

Joining rooms

Joining a room is just as easy as creating a room. We could modify our lobby example, so that clicking a room calls the `JoinRoom` function, such as:

```
foreach( RoomInfo room in PhotonNetwork.GetRoomList() )
{
  // if this room's join room button is clicked
  {
    PhotonNetwork.JoinRoom( room );
  }
}
```

Joining a room triggers the following callbacks:

- `OnJoinedRoom`, if the client has successfully connected to the given room.

- `OnPhotonJoinRoomFailed`, if the client could not join the room. Again, no parameters are provided, so it's impossible to know the exact cause, but the most likely reason is that either the room no longer exists, or it is full.

Filtering results by user preference

Many game lobbies allow players to filter the results by various criteria. For example, you might hide all private rooms, or only show rooms on a certain map.

Filtering arrays

We can filter out our room list array based on the user's preference, this way the user can more easily search for a suitable game to join:

```
using UnityEngine;
using System.Collections;
using System.Linq;
using System.Collections.Generic;

public class Example_FilterRooms
{
  public static RoomInfo[] FilterRooms( RoomInfo[] src, bool
    includeFull, Hashtable properties )
  {
    // use a Where expression to filter out rooms that do not
      match the given criteria
    // then convert that to an array
    return src.Where( room =>
      (
        filterRoom( room, includeFull, properties )
      ) ).ToArray();
  }

  private static bool filterRoom( RoomInfo src, bool includeFull,
    Hashtable properties )
  {
    // if includeFull is false, filter out the room if it's full
    bool include_full = ( src.playerCount >= src.maxPlayers
      || includeFull );

    // compare each custom property in the room for a match
    bool include_props = true;
```

```
    if( properties != null )
    {
      foreach( object key in properties )
      {
        // does not contain the key, therefore doesn't match our
          criteria
        if( !src.customProperties.ContainsKey( key ) )
        {
          include_props = false;
          break;
        }

        // value of key does not match, therefore doesn't match
          our criteria
        if( src.customProperties[ key ] != properties[ key ] )
        {
          include_props = false;
          break;
        }
      }
    }

    return include_full && include_props;
  }
}
```

If you haven't seen the => symbol before, it's a special expression which allows us to perform an operation on each element in an array. This is part of the **LINQ (Language Integrated Query)** feature of .NET. This is used in addition to methods such as Where, which evaluates a given Boolean expression per element and returns all elements which evaluate to true. In this case, we call a function per element which checks the room against the user's preferences, so only rooms which match the user's preferences are returned.

For more information about LINQ, see:

```
http://msdn.microsoft.com/en-us/library/vstudio/
bb397897.aspx
```

Filtering and caching a room list

Now we can call the preceding class's static `FilterRooms` function to get a filtered list of rooms.

Note that we probably do not want to call this every frame (or in the case of OnGUI, several times a frame), so instead of directly displaying the results of GetRoomList, we will wait until a room list is received, filter it, and cache the results. We can handle updates to the room list in the `OnReceivedRoomListUpdate` callback. Let's modify our connection/lobby script.

Whereas before we used:

```
foreach( RoomInfo room in PhotonNetwork.GetRoomList() )
{
  //...
}
```

We can now replace this with:

```
foreach( RoomInfo room in Example_FilterRooms.FilterRooms(
  PhotonNetwork.GetRoomList(), includeFullRooms,
  filterRoomProperties ) )
{
  //...
}
```

Where `includeFullRooms` indicates whether we want to include rooms in the search which are full to capacity, and `filterRoomProperties` is a hashtable of properties we want the room to match (for instance, what map we would like to play on).

Right now filtering doesn't serve any purpose (properties are null, and includeFull is true, so all rooms are included). However, these could be made public, and set by other scripts, or perhaps read from static fields.

Automatic matchmaking

Many games do not use a lobby. For example, console games often opt to randomly match players together rather than allowing them to browse a list of games (which could be unwieldy with a controller), or some games also have a "Quick Play" button in the lobby which allows the user to jump right into the action without having to browse the server lists. Usually, players can specify a preference, such as which map to play on, or what game mode they want.

Luckily, random matchmaking in PUN is very easy.

In PUN, you can call the `PhotonNetwork.JoinRandomRoom` function. This function takes a Hashtable of expected properties, and the desired max player count. It will attempt to join a random room, which will either call `OnJoinedRoom` if a room was found and the client was able to connect, or `OnPhotonRandomJoinFailed` if no room could be found (usually, this means all rooms are full, or no rooms are available).

Our lobby example might have a "Quick Play" button to do this:

```
// if quick play button is clicked
{
  // attempt to join a random room
  PhotonNetwork.JoinRoom( filterProperties, 0 );
}
```

If there are no rooms available to join, we can also start a new room.

```
void OnPhotonRandomJoinFailed()
{
  // failed to join a room, create a new one
  // passing a null name autogenerates a unique name.
  PhotonNetwork.CreateRoom( null, true, true, 8 );
}
```

Now the player can either manually find a room, or they can click the quick play button to immediately play. If no room is available, a new one is automatically created with a random name.

Finding friends

Let's say your game features a friends list, and you want to know if a friend is online or offline, or perhaps even want to join your friend if they are playing in a room. Luckily Photon Cloud recently added easy support for this via the `FindFriends` feature, which allows you to query the online states of a given list of users, as well the rooms the users are currently in, if any. The following example will locate and display a list of friends as defined in the inspector (in a real use case, these would likely be fetched from a database or some other source):

```
using UnityEngine;
using System.Collections;

public class Example_FindFriends : MonoBehaviour
{
```

```
public string[] Friends = new string[ 0 ];

void OnJoinedLobby()
{
  // Set our player name
  // Note that player names are not enforced to be unique. For
    the most part, this is used for screen names, but is also
    used for the FindFriends call
  // You can also change the name at any time
  PhotonNetwork.playerName = "TestPlayerName";

  // fetch the friends list from Photon
  // note that this is asynchronous, when the friends list is
    downloaded the results will be available via
    PhotonNetwork.Friends
  PhotonNetwork.FindFriends( Friends );
}

void OnGUI()
{
  if( !PhotonNetwork.connected )
    return;

  if( PhotonNetwork.Friends == null )
    return;


  foreach( FriendInfo friend in PhotonNetwork.Friends )
  {

    // display information about this friend
    // you can get the friend's name via friend.Name
    // friend.IsOnline is the online status of the friend
    // friend.IsInRoom indicates whether the friend is currently
      connected to a room
    // friend.Room indicates which room the friend is in, if any
  }

  GUILayout.EndArea();
}
}
```

In order for this to work, each player will need to set their name via `PhotonNetwork.playerName`. FindFriends will attempt to find the status of each friend by their username. There is no harm in including users that don't exist; they will simply show up as offline.

 Note that `FindFriends` cannot be called before connecting to the lobby. That is, calling `FindFriends` in `OnConnectedToPhoton` will result in an error, but `OnJoinedLobby` will work fine.

Syncing a level between players

In Unity Networking, we had to develop our own way to make sure each player was running on the same level, via RPCs, disabling the network queue, waiting for the load to finish, and so on.

In Photon, this problem is significantly easier to solve. You simply set `PhotonNetwork.automaticallySyncScene` to true, and to load a level call `PhotonNetwork.LoadLevel` on the master client. For example, we can modify our lobby example to automatically sync the scene between players in a room.

Firstly, in `Start` we would enable automatic level syncing:

```
void Start()
{
  // ...
  // ensure that all players play on the same map
  PhotonNetwork.automaticallySyncScene = true;
}
```

Then, when starting a game, we use PhotonNetwork's load level replacement in order to load the level for all players:

```
void OnCreatedRoom()
{
  PhotonNetwork.LoadLevel( "Level Name Here" );
}
```

Note that level loads can also occur in-game. For example, this feature makes it incredibly easy to add a map vote feature, where players can vote for the next map, and at the end of the round the map with the most votes is loaded.

Creating a chat client

We're going to put what we've learned about Photon to use, creating a chat client from scratch. Players can choose from a list of running chatrooms, create a new chatroom, or join a random chatroom (if there are none available, one is created). While in a chatroom, players can chat with everybody in the chatroom. From the main menu, players can also manage a list of "friends" (they can add and remove names). They can see the online states of each friend, as well as join friends if they are in a room.

The Connect screen

The first screen the user is presented with is the **Connect** screen.

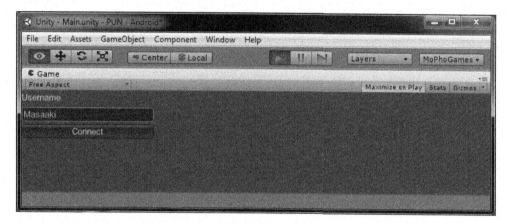

Here, they enter their username and connect to Photon. It will automatically remember the last username they entered, since they are likely to want to use it again.

This script accomplishes the **Connect** screen. This goes on an empty game object. After the user connects, it will disable itself and activate the lobby screen on another game object:

```
using UnityEngine;
using System.Collections;

public class ConnectToPhoton : MonoBehaviour
{
  public GameObject LobbyScreen;

  private string username = "";
```

```
private bool connecting = false;
private string error = null;

void Start()
{
  // load the last username the player entered
  username = PlayerPrefs.GetString( "Username", "" );
}

void OnGUI()
{
  // in the process of connecting...
  if( connecting )
  {
    GUILayout.Label( "Connecting..." );
    return;
  }

  // an error occurred, display it
  if( error != null )
  {
    GUILayout.Label( "Failed to connect: " + error );
    return;
  }

  // let the user enter their username
  GUILayout.Label( "Username" );
  username = GUILayout.TextField( username, GUILayout.Width(
    200f ) );

  if( GUILayout.Button( "Connect" ) )
  {
    // remember username for next time
    PlayerPrefs.SetString( "Username", username );

    // in the process of connecting
    connecting = true;

    // set username, connect to photon
    PhotonNetwork.playerName = username;
    PhotonNetwork.ConnectUsingSettings( "v1.0" );
  }
}
```

```
void OnJoinedLobby()
{
  // joined the lobby, show lobby screen

  connecting = false;
  gameObject. SetActiveRecursively ( false );
  LobbyScreen. SetActiveRecursively ( true );
}

void OnFailedToConnectToPhoton( DisconnectCause cause )
{
  // failed to connect, store error for display

  connecting = false;
  error = cause.ToString();
}
}
```

Right now, if you run this, you can enter your username and connect. It will then display **Connecting...** until it connects, or an error occurs. If an error occurs it will be displayed. Otherwise, the message goes away and we're left with a blank screen. You'll also notice a null reference exception in the console, as our lobby screen is not yet defined. Let's remedy these by creating our lobby script.

The Lobby screen

The lobby screen will allow the user to join a random game, host a game, or browse available games to manually join. We'll also add a button that will show the user's friends list, for now it won't do anything.

 Earlier in this chapter, we covered filtering room lists by preference. A good use case for our chatroom might be to allow players to specify a language upon creating a room. For instance, add buttons for English, Spanish, or French. The room could be created with a Language key containing the user-specified language. This can then be filtered in the Lobby, so the user could either select All, English, Spanish, or French to join rooms of a specific language.

```
using UnityEngine;
using System.Collections;

public class LobbyScreen : MonoBehaviour
{
  Vector2 lobbyScroll = Vector2.zero;
```

```
void Awake()
{
  // as explained before, we use automaticallySyncScene to
    ensure all players load the same level automatically
  PhotonNetwork.automaticallySyncScene = true;
}


void OnGUI()
{
  // allow the player to join a random room if they don't feel
    like browsing room lists
  if( GUILayout.Button( "Join Random", GUILayout.Width( 200f ) )
    )
  {
    PhotonNetwork.JoinRandomRoom();
  }

  // create a new room
  if( GUILayout.Button( "Create Room", GUILayout.Width( 200f ) )
    )
  {
    // create a room with the user's name, visible in the lobby,
      allow other players to join, maximum of 32 players
      allowed.
    PhotonNetwork.CreateRoom( PlayerPrefs.GetString( "Username"
      ) + "'s Room", true, true, 32 );
  }

  // TODO: show the friends list management page
  GUILayout.Button( "Friends", GUILayout.Width( 200f ) );

  // get a list of rooms currently open
  RoomInfo[] rooms = PhotonNetwork.GetRoomList();
  // no rooms available, inform the user
  if( rooms.Length == 0 )
  {
    GUILayout.Label( "No Rooms Available" );
  }
  else
  {
    // show a scrollable list of rooms

    lobbyScroll = GUILayout.BeginScrollView( lobbyScroll,
      GUILayout.Width( 220f ), GUILayout.ExpandHeight( true ) );
```

```
      // iterate over each room and display a line for that room,
        in addition to an "Enter" button
      foreach( RoomInfo room in PhotonNetwork.GetRoomList() )
      {
        GUILayout.BeginHorizontal( GUILayout.Width( 200f ) );

        // display room name and number of players / capacity
        GUILayout.Label( room.name + " - " + room.playerCount +
          "/" + room.maxPlayers );

        // connect to the room if the player clicks the "Enter"
          button
        if( GUILayout.Button( "Enter" ) )
        {
          PhotonNetwork.JoinRoom( room );
        }

        GUILayout.EndHorizontal();
      }

      GUILayout.EndScrollView();
    }
  }

  // if no room could be randomly joined, create a new room
  void OnPhotonRandomJoinFailed()
  {
    // create a new room with the player's name, visible to the
      lobby, open to other players, maximum of 32 players.
    PhotonNetwork.CreateRoom( PlayerPrefs.GetString( "Username" )
      + "'s Room", true, true, 32 );
  }

  // after creating the room, load the chat room scene
  void OnCreatedRoom()
  {
    // load the chatroom scene via PhotonNetwork.LoadLevel, this
      way everyone who joins will automatically load the level.
    PhotonNetwork.LoadLevel( "ChatRoom" );
  }
}
```

Attach this to an empty game object, drag the game object onto the **LobbyScreen** slot of the **Connect** script, and deactivate the lobby screen game object.

The chat room

Note that either Join Random or Create Room will both result in an error, that the "ChatRoom" scene does not exist. Let's find a remedy to this.

Save the current scene as `Main` and add it to the build settings. Then, create a new scene, save it as `ChatRoom`, and add it to the build settings as well.

Now we can create our chatroom script and add it to this scene shown as follows:

```
using UnityEngine;
using System.Collections;
using System.Collections.Generic;

public class Chatbox : Photon.MonoBehaviour
{
  // keep up to this many messages, after which older messages
    start to be deleted
  public int MaxMessages = 100;

  private Vector2 chatScroll = Vector2.zero;
  private List<string> chatMessages = new List<string>();

  private string message = "";

  void OnGUI()
  {
    if( GUILayout.Button( "Leave Room" ) )
    {
      // leave the room we're in
      PhotonNetwork.LeaveRoom();
    }

    // display a scrolling list of chat messages
    chatScroll = GUILayout.BeginScrollView( chatScroll,
      GUILayout.Width( Screen.width ), GUILayout.ExpandHeight(
      true ) );

    foreach( string msg in chatMessages )
    {
      GUILayout.Label( msg );
    }
```

```
    GUILayout.EndScrollView();

    GUILayout.BeginHorizontal();

    // let the user type a message
    message = GUILayout.TextField( message, GUILayout.ExpandWidth(
      true ) );

    if( GUILayout.Button( "Send", GUILayout.Width( 100f ) ) )
    {
      // tell everybody to add this message
      photonView.RPC( "AddChat", PhotonTargets.All, message );
      message = "";
    }

    GUILayout.EndHorizontal();
  }

  [RPC]
  void AddChat( string message, PhotonMessageInfo info )
  {
    // store the received message
    chatMessages.Add( info.sender.name + ": " + message );

    // enforce maximum stored messages
    if( chatMessages.Count > MaxMessages )
    {
      chatMessages.RemoveAt( 0 );
    }

    // set scroll Y to a really big value
    // Unity will automatically clamp this, having the effect of
scrolling to the bottom
    chatScroll.y = 10000;
  }

  // if the user leaves, go back to the main scene
  void OnLeftRoom()
  {
    Application.LoadLevel( "Main" );
  }
}
```

What happens here is that the user is allowed to type a message. On clicking the **Send** button this message is passed to an RPC (`PhotonTargets.All` will call the RPC for every player in the room). This RPC will add the new message, prefixed with the player name (`PhotonMessageInfo.sender.name` is the name of the player who sent the RPC), to the list of messages (which it also limits to a maximum count), and scroll the chatbox to the bottom.

Our chat script is now fully functional. Next, we're going to add the friends list functionality to our chatroom app.

Adding friends lists

Players can add and remove friends from the main menu. They can also view a list of friends, online states, and optionally join their friends if the friend is inside a chatroom. The actual list of friends is persisted to PlayerPrefs as a comma-delimited string:

```
using UnityEngine;
using System.Collections;
using System.Collections.Generic;

public class FriendsScreen : MonoBehaviour
{
  public GameObject LobbyScreen;

  private string addFriendName = "";

  private List<string> friends = new List<string>();

  private Dictionary<string, bool> onlineStates = new
    Dictionary<string, bool>();
  private Dictionary<string, string> rooms = new
    Dictionary<string, string>();

  void Awake()
  {
    // load friends from PlayerPrefs
    string stored_friends = PlayerPrefs.GetString( "FriendsList",
      "" );
    if( !string.IsNullOrEmpty( stored_friends ) )
    {
      friends.AddRange( stored_friends.Split( ',' ) );
    }

    // request friend states
```

```
    if( friends.Count > 0 )
    {
      PhotonNetwork.FindFriends( friends.ToArray() );
    }
}

void OnGUI()
{
  // go back to the lobby screen
  if( GUILayout.Button( "Back", GUILayout.Width( 200f ) ) )
  {
    gameObject. SetActiveRecursively ( false );
    LobbyScreen. SetActiveRecursively ( true );
  }

  GUILayout.Label( "Add Friend:" );

  GUILayout.BeginHorizontal();

  // let the player type in a friend name
  addFriendName = GUILayout.TextField( addFriendName,
    GUILayout.Width( 200f ) );

  // add player name to friends list, request friend states
  if( GUILayout.Button( "Add", GUILayout.Width( 100f ) ) )
  {
    AddFriend( addFriendName );
  }

  GUILayout.EndHorizontal();

  if( PhotonNetwork.Friends != null )
  {
    foreach( FriendInfo friend in PhotonNetwork.Friends )
    {
      GUILayout.BeginHorizontal();

      GUILayout.Label( friend.Name + " [" + ( GetOnlineState(
        friend ) ? "Online]" : "Offline]" ) );

      if( GetIsInRoom( friend ) )
      {
```

```
        if( GUILayout.Button( "Join", GUILayout.Width( 50f ) ) )
        {
          // join the friend in whatever room they are in
          PhotonNetwork.JoinRoom( GetRoom( friend ) );
        }
      }

      // remove the friend from the friends list, and fetch
        friend states
      if( GUILayout.Button( "Remove", GUILayout.Width( 100f )
        )
      {
        RemoveFriend( friend.Name );
      }

      GUILayout.EndHorizontal();
    }
  }
}

void Update()
{
  if( PhotonNetwork.FriendsListAge >= 1000 )
  {
    PhotonNetwork.FindFriends( friends.ToArray() );
  }
}

// while updating a friends list, Photon will temporarily set
  isOnline and isInRoom to false
// if you update on a timer, you will notice state rapidly
  switching between offline and online
// therefore, we will store online state and room in a
  dictionary and wait until an update is actually received
// and store the updated value
void OnUpdatedFriendList()
{
  foreach( FriendInfo friend in PhotonNetwork.Friends )
  {
    onlineStates[ friend.Name ] = friend.IsOnline;
    rooms[ friend.Name ] = friend.IsInRoom ? friend.Room : "";
  }
}

bool GetOnlineState( FriendInfo friend )
{
```

```
    if( onlineStates.ContainsKey( friend.Name ) )
      return onlineStates[ friend.Name ];
    else
      return false;
  }

  bool GetIsInRoom( FriendInfo friend )
  {
    if( rooms.ContainsKey( friend.Name ) )
      return !string.IsNullOrEmpty( rooms[ friend.Name ] );
    else
      return false;
  }

  string GetRoom( FriendInfo friend )
  {
    if( rooms.ContainsKey( friend.Name ) )
      return rooms[ friend.Name ];
    else
      return "";
  }

  void AddFriend( string friendName )
  {
    friends.Add( friendName );
    PhotonNetwork.FindFriends( friends.ToArray() );

    // save friends to PlayerPrefs
    PlayerPrefs.SetString( "FriendsList", string.Join( ",",
      friends.ToArray() ) );
  }

  void RemoveFriend( string friendName )
  {
    friends.Remove( friendName );
    PhotonNetwork.FindFriends( friends.ToArray() );

    // save friends to PlayerPrefs
    PlayerPrefs.SetString( "FriendsList", string.Join( ",",
      friends.ToArray() ) );
  }
}
```

Place this script on an empty game object, and deactivate the game object. Drag the lobby screen game object onto the **LobbyScreen** slot.

Finally, let's modify our lobby script to go to the friends list screen.

Firstly, we'll add a reference to the friends list object:

```
public GameObject FriendsListScreen;
```

And in OnGUI, we'll add a button to display the friends list:

```
if( GUILayout.Button( "Friends", GUILayout.Width( 200 ) ) )
{
  gameObject.SetActiveRecursively( false );
  FriendsListScreen.SetActiveRecursively( true );
}
```

 Note that as of Unity 4, SetActiveRecursively is deprecated. You should instead use SetActive. However, this function does not exist in Unity 3.

Drag the friends list game object onto the new **FriendsListScreen** slot.

The chatbox example is now completely functional.

Summary

In this chapter, we learned what Photon Unity Networking does differently to Unity Networking and how to use PhotonViews. We learned to get a list of rooms in the lobby, filtered by user preference, and how to create and join rooms as well as how to add random matchmaking. We learned how to add friends list features, and making sure everyone plays on the same level.

We also applied these concepts to create a fully functional chat client. Players can create or join, manage a list of friends, and of course, chat with others.

In the next chapter, we will be exploring another networking technology from ExitGames, called Photon Server.

3
Photon Server – Star Collector

In the last chapter, we covered Photon Unity Networking, coupled with Photon Cloud. In this chapter, we'll be covering another multiplayer technology from Exit Games, called Photon Server.

Photon Server is a dedicated server middleware. That means, unlike Unity Networking or Photon Unity Networking, games are not organized by players (in rooms or hosts). Instead, players connect to a single dedicated server, which is in charge of processing game logic. This is the kind of setup you would see in an MMO (for example, a single region in the game might be a server).

In this chapter we will cover the following topics:

- What differs Photon Server from Photon Unity Networking or Unity Networking
- Getting the Photon Server
- Setting up a Photon Server instance
- Setting up the Photon Client SDK in Unity
- Creating a new server application
- Connecting and sending/receiving messages
- Creating a central game logic class
- Assigning player IDs
- Creating a semi-server-authoritative Star Collector game
- Let's get started.

Dedicated servers

Photon Server is built on the concept of dedicated servers. Whereas in Unity Networking one player is the host and other players directly connect to their machine, in Photon Server you host one or more dedicated servers that players connect to. Additionally, this server usually performs as much game logic as possible, unlike Photon Unity Networking /Photon Cloud, where clients are responsible for game logic.

Dedicated servers are most often used for MMO-type games, as mentioned previously. By processing as much logic on the server as possible, the potential for cheating is dramatically reduced. For example, many MMOs implement simple point-and-click movement logic, where the player simply points where they want to move to. The client would most likely send a simple move request containing the point the user clicked. The server handles path finding and actually moving the character to that point. The client can also predict how the character will move (by generating its own path and moving the character), but ultimately the server gets total control over the character (and likely broadcasts an absolute position often, which the client "corrects" as its own state, to ensure the client is always in step with the server).

Photon Server also includes a redistributable package. This allows players to host their own servers, similar to games like Minecraft (where the server logic is separated into another application, which is running with the game). This can be an improvement over games hosted within the client, as players can run their server on a dedicated machine without playing actively.

Getting the Photon Server

Assuming that you've created an ExitGames account (as detailed in the last chapter), you can visit this page: `https://www.exitgames.com/Download`, for downloading client and server SDKs:

Download the first link, the Photon Server SDK exe. This is a self-extracting archive, so after downloading simply browse to the location you want to extract the server code to.

You'll also want to download the Unity3D SDK, so find the download link among the list of client SDKs and download it.

After downloading the client SDK, navigate to **libs** | **Release** and drop the `Photon3Unity3D.dll` file into a **Plugins** folder in your Unity project.

You will also want to download the server license file, so choose the first on the download page (100 CCU, no expiry) and drop it into the **deploy | bin_win32** directory of your server application. To run the Photon Server, simply run PhotonControl.exe. It's not ready to connect as—first, we need to create our own server application.

Creating a server application

Let's create a new server application. Upon receiving any message, it will simply get an echo, a confirmation that it has received the message (an acknowledgement).

Creating a class library

Create a new class library project called PhotonAckServer. I have put mine in the src-server directory.

Now, we'll add three references to our project. These can be found in the **libs** directory of the Photon Server:

- ExitGamesLibs.dll
- Photon.SocketServer.dll
- PhotonHostRuntimeInterfaces.dll

With these added, create a new PhotonAckServer class. This will inherit from ApplicationBase, code for the same is as follows:

```
using Photon.SocketServer;

public class PhotonAckServer : ApplicationBase
{
  protected override PeerBase CreatePeer( InitRequest initRequest
    )
  {
  }

  protected override void Setup()
  {
  }

  protected override void TearDown()
  {
  }
}
```

And we'll also create a new `PhotonAckPeer` class as follows:

```
using Photon.SocketServer;
using PhotonHostRuntimeInterfaces;

class PhotonAckPeer : PeerBase
{
  public PhotonAckPeer( IRpcProtocol protocol, IPhotonPeer
    unmanagedPeer )
    : base( protocol, unmanagedPeer )
  {
  }

  protected override void OnDisconnect( DisconnectReason
    reasonCode, string reasonDetail )
  {
  }

  protected override void OnOperationRequest( OperationRequest
    operationRequest, SendParameters sendParameters )
  {
  }
  }
}
```

And modify our `PhotonAckServer` to return the `PhotonAckPeer` we just created:

```
using Photon.SocketServer;
public class PhotonAckServer : ApplicationBase
{
  protected override PeerBase CreatePeer( InitRequest initRequest
    )
  {
    return new PhotonAckPeer( initRequest.Protocol,
      initRequest.PhotonPeer );
  }

  protected override void Setup()
  {
  }

  protected override void TearDown()
  {
  }
}
```

So, what did we just do here? We have created a class library (which compiles down to a DLL). This is known as a server application. It is in charge of handling all server-side logic in Photon. It compiles to a DLL, which is referenced by the actual Photon Server EXE.

This setup involves at least two classes, an Application and a Peer. The Application class isn't much more than glue code, creating and returning a new instance of our Peer class (it can also handle startup and shutdown if need be) when requested.

The Peer class essentially wraps a specific client (when a client connects, the Application class will create and return a new peer for that client). It can handle messages coming from the client (known as operation requests), and can send messages back to the client (either as responses to operation requests, or as events, which don't need to be in response to anything).

Responding to operation requests

So, let's send our "ack" as a response. First, we'll create an enum variable of values, which map to response codes using following code:

```
public enum PhotonAckResponseTypes : byte
{
  Ack = 0
}
```

Right now there is only one entry, but we can easily add more responsive codes by adding the enum variable values (the point of using an enum variable value is for organization and more readable code)

Now, in our PhotonAckPeer, let's modify our OnOperationRequest function to return an ack response.

```
using Photon.SocketServer;
using PhotonHostRuntimeInterfaces;
using System.Collections.Generic;

class PhotonAckPeer : PeerBase
{
  public PhotonAckPeer( IRpcProtocol protocol, IPhotonPeer
    unmanagedPeer )
    : base( protocol, unmanagedPeer )
  {
  }
```

```
protected override void OnDisconnect( DisconnectReason
  reasonCode, string reasonDetail )
{

}

protected override void OnOperationRequest( OperationRequest
  operationRequest, SendParameters sendParameters )
{
  // send an "ack" back to the client
  OperationResponse response = new OperationResponse(
    (byte)PhotonAckResponseTypes.Ack );
  this.SendOperationResponse( response, sendParameters );
}
}
```

Deploying the server code

Although this is a very simple example, we've now got a fully functional server application. To build this, first ensure that the built server DLL is placed under your project's directory under **bin** (this is required by the Photon Server application), now start to build the project.

Copy the bin folder you just built to the deploy folder under deploy/ PhotonAckServer/. Now ,we'll need to edit the Photon Server configuration to ensure that it knows about our new application. The configuration file is located at deploy/bin_win32/PhotonServer.config. You should see a section titled Applications. Add the following entry:

```
<Application
  Name="PhotonAckServer"
  BaseDirectory="PhotonAckServer"
  Assembly="PhotonAckServer"
  Type="PhotonAckServer">
</Application>
```

Now, our server is ready to handle clients. Let's make a client in Unity, which will send and receive messages from Photon.

Connecting from Unity and passing messages

Connecting to a Photon Server from Unity is very simple. You just need to specify the IP, port, and application which you want to use (in this case, we will specify `PhotonAckServer` as the application). Each application defined in the Photon Server configuration will run alongside each other—this lets you run a number of different server types such as master servers and game servers on a single physical machine.

Let's create a script to connect to Photon, service the connection ten times per second, and sends a test message to the server (which responds with an acknowledgement message).

First, we'll start with this:

```
using UnityEngine;
using System.Collections;
using ExitGames.Client.Photon;

public class PhotonAckClient : MonoBehaviour, IPhotonPeerListener
{
}
```

We'll add some variables to the top of the script:

```
public PhotonPeer peer;
private bool connected = false;
```

In Start, we'll connect to the server and kick off a co-routine, which services the connection:

```
public void Start()
{
  // connect to Photon server
  peer = new PhotonPeer( this, ConnectionProtocol.Udp );
  peer.Connect( "127.0.0.1:5055", "PhotonAckServer" );

  StartCoroutine( doService() );
}
```

Our service co-routine calls service and then delays for 0.1 seconds, in a while loop:

```
IEnumerator doService()
{
  while( true )
  {
```

```
      peer.Service();
      yield return new WaitForSeconds( 0.1f );
    }
  }
```

We'll also implement some methods required by the `IPhotonPeerListener`
interface:

```csharp
#region IPhotonPeerListener Members

public void DebugReturn( DebugLevel level, string message )
{
  // log message to console
  Debug.Log( message );
}

public void OnEvent( EventData eventData )
{
  //server raised an event
  Debug.Log( "Received event - type: " + eventData.Code.ToString()
    );
}

public void OnOperationResponse( OperationResponse operationResponse )
{
  //server sent operation response
  Debug.Log( "Received op response - type: " +
    operationResponse.OperationCode.ToString() );
}

public void OnStatusChanged( StatusCode statusCode )
{
  // connected to Photon server
  if( statusCode == StatusCode.Connect )
  {
    connected = true;
  }

  // log status change
  Debug.Log( "Status change: " + statusCode.ToString() );
}

#endregion
```

Finally, we'll display a GUI with a button that sends a test message to the server using the following code:

```
void OnGUI()
{
  GUILayout.Label( "Connected: " + connected.ToString() );

  if( connected )
  {
    if( GUILayout.Button( "Send Operation Request" ) )
    {
      // send a message to the server
      peer.OpCustom( 0, new System.Collections.Generic.
        Dictionary<byte, object>(), true );
    }
  }
}
```

So, what exactly does this script accomplish?

- It creates a new `PhotonPeer` class, which represents a connection to the Photon Server instance. It passes itself to the constructor, which causes the `PhotonPeer` class to call the `IPhotonPeerListener` methods that our class implements. It also specifies to use UDP for communication. This lets you specify which messages are reliable, and which are unreliable.

- It calls the service method of our `PhotonPeer` ten times per second. This causes the `PhotonPeer` class to process incoming messages and send outgoing messages. In a twitch-based game, this should be called more often to reduce lag (twenty times per second should suffice).

- It displays the connection status in OnGUI. If connected, it also shows a button, which will cause a test message to be sent to the server (via the `OpCustom` method of the `PhotonPeer` class, which sends an operation request to the server).

- It implements the `DebugReturn`, `OnEvent`, and `OnOperationResponse` methods to log the values to the console.

- It implements the `OnStatusChange` method to detect when the PhotonPeer class has successfully established a connection.

This is really all that is needed for basic communication with a Photon Server. You can handle connection/disconnection with `OnStatusChange`, send messages to the server with the `OpCustom` method, and receive messages with `OnOperationResponse` and `OnEvent`.

Creating a game logic class

When writing game servers, it's very common that you need some central class for processing game logic. What we have right now doesn't allow for that, so we're going to modify our `ack` server to add a central class for processing game logic.

Our game class will accomplish the same thing that our `ack` server already does (sends acknowledgements in response to operation requests). It will also be able to keep track of a list of peers connected to the server, and when the server shuts down it will automatically disconnect any peers that are currently connected.

```
using Photon.SocketServer;
using PhotonHostRuntimeInterfaces;

using System.Collections.Generic;

public class PhotonAckGame
{
  public static PhotonAckGame Instance;

  public List<PeerBase> Connections;

  public void Startup()
  {
    Connections = new List<PeerBase>();
  }

  public void Shutdown()
  {
    // kick out any players still on the server before shutting
      down
    foreach( PeerBase peer in Connections )
    {
      peer.Disconnect();
    }
  }

  public void PeerConnected( PeerBase peer )
  {
    lock( Connections )
    {
      Connections.Add( peer );
    }
  }
```

```
public void PeerDisconnected( PeerBase peer )
{
  lock( Connections )
  {
    Connections.Remove( peer );
  }
}

public void OnOperationRequest( PeerBase src, OperationRequest
  request, SendParameters sendParams )
{
  // send ack to peer
  src.SendOperationResponse( new OperationResponse(
    (byte)PhotonAckResponseTypes.Ack ), sendParams );
}
}
```

 Note the use of lock statements—peers in Photon Server are executed in parallel for performance. This presents thread safety issues, so you need to be careful to properly deal with thread safety.

In our `Application` class, in the `Setup` method we'll create a new instance of the game and call its `Startup` method. Additionally, in the `Teardown` method, we'll call the game instance's `Shutdown` method.

```
using Photon.SocketServer;

public class PhotonAckServer : ApplicationBase
{
  protected override PeerBase CreatePeer( InitRequest initRequest
    )
  {
    return new PhotonAckPeer( initRequest.Protocol,
      initRequest.PhotonPeer );
  }

  protected override void Setup()
  {
    PhotonAckGame.Instance = new PhotonAckGame();
    PhotonAckGame.Instance.Startup();
  }

  protected override void TearDown()
```

```
        {
            PhotonAckGame.Instance.Shutdown();
        }
    }
```

And finally, in our peer class we need to inform the game instance of connecting peers, disconnecting peers, and operation requests.

```
using Photon.SocketServer;
using PhotonHostRuntimeInterfaces;
using System.Collections.Generic;

class PhotonAckPeer : PeerBase
{
    public PhotonAckPeer( IRpcProtocol protocol, IPhotonPeer
        unmanagedPeer )
        : base( protocol, unmanagedPeer )
    {
        PhotonAckGame.Instance.PeerConnected( this );
    }

    protected override void OnDisconnect( DisconnectReason
        reasonCode, string reasonDetail )
    {
        PhotonAckGame.Instance.PeerDisconnected( this );
    }

    protected override void OnOperationRequest( OperationRequest
        operationRequest, SendParameters sendParameters )
    {
        PhotonAckGame.Instance.OnOperationRequest( this,
            operationRequest, sendParameters );
    }
}
```

If you run this server and connect from Unity, you should have the same results as you did before, but the difference is that we are now processing messages from a central class rather than on a per-peer basis, which makes designing server logic for multiplayers far easier.

Assigning player IDs

Another feature required by nearly all multiplayer games, is the ability to track players by player ID. We need some kind of lightweight data, which uniquely identifies a specific player, such as a number (for instance, an object might store this number as a reference to the player who owns it). So, let's modify our server to assign player IDs to peers as they connect. It will also notify the client of its player ID upon connecting.

We'll use a long integer for the purpose.

A static long variable is initialized with the smallest value possible (long.MinValue), the last assigned player ID. When a player joins, we copy the static variable as their ID, and then increment the static variable.

```
using Photon.SocketServer;
using PhotonHostRuntimeInterfaces;
using System.Collections.Generic;

class PhotonAckPeer : PeerBase
{
  // note that we use long.MinValue rather than zero. Signed integer
  values have a negative minimum and positive maximum. Starting at
  zero divides the possible range of IDs in half, but starting at
  the lowest possible value gives us the largest possible range.
  private static long lastAssignedPlayerID = long.MinValue;
  private static object lockPlayerID = new object();

  public long PlayerID;

  public PhotonAckPeer( IRpcProtocol protocol, IPhotonPeer
    unmanagedPeer )
    : base( protocol, unmanagedPeer )
  {
    lock( lockPlayerID )
    {
      this.PlayerID = lastAssignedPlayerID;
      lastAssignedPlayerID++;
    }
    PhotonAckGame.Instance.PeerConnected( this );
  }

  protected override void OnDisconnect( DisconnectReason
    reasonCode, string reasonDetail )
  {
    PhotonAckGame.Instance.PeerDisconnected( this );
```

```
    }

    protected override void OnOperationRequest( OperationRequest
      operationRequest, SendParameters sendParameters )
    {
      PhotonAckGame.Instance.OnOperationRequest( this,
        operationRequest, sendParameters );
    }
  }
```

Now, our peer has a player ID but the client doesn't know what their player ID is. Let's create an event type enum variable instance (just as we did for the response type enum), since we'll send an event to the peer containing the peer's assigned player ID.

```
public enum PhotonAckEventType : byte
{
  AssignPlayerID = 0
}
```

And in our peer constructor, send an event with the AssignPlayerID event type:

```
using Photon.SocketServer;
using PhotonHostRuntimeInterfaces;
using System.Collections.Generic;

class PhotonAckPeer : PeerBase
{
  private static long lastAssignedPlayerID = long.MinValue;
  private static object lockPlayerID = new object();

  public ulong PlayerID;

  public PhotonAckPeer( IRpcProtocol protocol,
    IPhotonPeer unmanagedPeer )
    : base( protocol, unmanagedPeer )
  {
    lock( lockPlayerID )
    {
      this.PlayerID = lastAssignedPlayerID;
      lastAssignedPlayerID++;
    }

    PhotonAckGame.Instance.PeerConnected( this );

    EventData evt = new EventData(
      (byte)PhotonAckEventType.AssignPlayerID );
```

```
        evt.Parameters = new Dictionary<byte, object>() { { 0,
          this.PlayerID } };
        this.SendEvent( evt, new SendParameters() );
    }

    protected override void OnDisconnect( DisconnectReason
      reasonCode, string reasonDetail )
    {
        PhotonAckGame.Instance.PeerDisconnected( this );
    }

    protected override void OnOperationRequest( OperationRequest
      operationRequest, SendParameters sendParameters )
    {
        PhotonAckGame.Instance.OnOperationRequest( this,
          operationRequest, sendParameters );
    }
}
```

Now, copy the `PhotonAckEventTypes` file to our Unity project, and we'll modify our Unity client to receive and store player ID from the `OnEvent` function:

```
public void OnEvent( EventData eventData )
{
    //server raised an event
    Debug.Log( "Received event - type: " + eventData.Code.ToString() );

    if( (PhotonAckEventType)eventData.Code ==
      PhotonAckEventType.AssignPlayerID )
    {
        long playerID = (long)eventData.Parameters[ 0 ];
        Debug.Log( "Received player ID: " + playerID );
        localPlayerID = playerID;
    }
}
```

Now, upon connecting you will see that it has received the player ID in the console.

We're now going to use these concepts to build a star collector game in Photon.

Building a star collector game

Our star collector game will be a semi-server-authoritative game. That is, players send move commands (which makes it possible to speedhack, teleport, and so on) but the server gets control over spawning players, stars, controlling star pickup, and other game logic.

Upon joining the server, players are spawned. Players will find stars they can collect. When all stars have been collected, the winner is announced in chat based on the player with the most stars, the stars are re-spawned, and the players reset.

Preparing the class library

Again, we're going to make a class library for our game server. This class library, as before, contains the `Peer` class and the `Application` class.

 You may find it easier, if you will work with Photon frequently, to create a project template in Visual Studio, so you already have a base to work from instead of recreating the project from scratch each time.

We'll also create a `Game` class just as we did with the `Ack` server.

```
using Photon.SocketServer;
using PhotonHostRuntimeInterfaces;

using System.Collections.Generic;

namespace StarCollectorDemo
{
  public class StarCollectorDemoGame
  {
    public static StarCollectorDemoGame Instance;

    public void Startup()
    {
    }

    public void Shutdown()
    {
    }

    public void PeerJoined( StarCollectorDemoPeer peer )
    {
```

```
        }

        public void PeerLeft( StarCollectorDemoPeer peer )
        {
        }

        public void OnOperationRequest( StarCollectorDemoPeer sender,
            OperationRequest operationRequest, SendParameters
            sendParameters )
        {
        }
    }
}
```

And, we'll create a new instance of the Game class when our application starts up:

```
using Photon.SocketServer;
using PhotonHostRuntimeInterfaces;

namespace StarCollectorDemo
{
    public class StarCollectorDemoApplication : ApplicationBase
    {
        protected override PeerBase CreatePeer( InitRequest
            initRequest )
        {
            return new StarCollectorDemoPeer( initRequest.Protocol,
                initRequest.PhotonPeer );
        }

        protected override void Setup()
        {
            StarCollectorDemoGame.Instance = new
                StarCollectorDemoGame();
            StarCollectorDemoGame.Instance.Startup();
        }

        protected override void TearDown()
        {
            StarCollectorDemoGame.Instance.Shutdown();
        }
    }
}
```

And finally, we'll also hook up our `Peer` class to the `Game` class:

```
using Photon.SocketServer;
using PhotonHostRuntimeInterfaces;

namespace StarCollectorDemo
{
  public class StarCollectorDemoPeer : PeerBase
  {
    public StarCollectorDemoPeer( IRpcProtocol protocol,
      IPhotonPeer unmanagedPeer )
      : base( protocol, unmanagedPeer )
    {
      lock( StarCollectorDemoGame.Instance )
      {
        StarCollectorDemoGame.Instance.PeerJoined( this );
      }
    }

    protected override void OnDisconnect( DisconnectReason
      reasonCode, string reasonDetail )
    {
      lock( StarCollectorDemoGame.Instance )
      {
        StarCollectorDemoGame.Instance.PeerLeft( this );
      }
    }

    protected override void OnOperationRequest( OperationRequest
      operationRequest, SendParameters sendParameters )
    {
      StarCollectorDemoGame.Instance.OnOperationRequest( this,
        operationRequest, sendParameters );
    }
  }
}
```

Before we move on to actually creating the game logic, we're going to make one important change: We need to create some kind of message queue for our `Game` class, so that it can thread-safely process messages. We're going to use a handy class provided with Photon called `PoolFiber`.

What does this do? Well, when our Game class starts up we'll create a new
PoolFiber instance. When a message is received, we call our PoolFiber instance's
Enqueue method, queuing a new action, which calls a ProcessMessage function. The
PoolFiber class is essentially a way for other threads to schedule actions to be called
on the main thread. So, we'll use this as a way for peer threads to schedule messages
to be processed on the main thread.

So, here's what our Game class will look like:

```
using Photon.SocketServer;
using PhotonHostRuntimeInterfaces;
using ExitGames.Concurrency.Fibers;

using System.Collections.Generic;

namespace StarCollectorDemo
{
  public class StarCollectorDemoGame
  {
    public static StarCollectorDemoGame Instance;

    private IFiber executionFiber;

    public void Startup()
    {
      // create a new execution fiber and start it
      executionFiber = new PoolFiber();
      executionFiber.Start();
    }

    public void Shutdown()
    {
      // dispose the execution fiber
      executionFiber.Dispose();
    }

    public void PeerJoined( StarCollectorDemoPeer peer )
    {
    }

    public void PeerLeft( StarCollectorDemoPeer peer )
    {
    }
```

```
public void OnOperationRequest( StarCollectorDemoPeer sender,
  OperationRequest operationRequest, SendParameters
  sendParameters )
{

  // schedule a message to be processed on the main thread
  executionFiber.Enqueue( () => { this.ProcessMessage( sender,
    operationRequest, sendParameters ); } );
}

public void ProcessMessage( StarCollectorDemoPeer sender,
  OperationRequest operationRequest, SendParameters
  sendParameters )
{
  // process messages here
}
  }
}
```

Now, we can safely process messages in our `ProcessMessage` function without worrying about thread safety.

We can also use this for other features. For example, let's keep a list of all peers connected to the game. We'll use the execution fiber to schedule `Add` and `Remove` operations on a `List` object:

```
using Photon.SocketServer;
using PhotonHostRuntimeInterfaces;
using ExitGames.Concurrency.Fibers;

using System.Collections.Generic;

namespace StarCollectorDemo
{
  public class StarCollectorDemoGame
  {
    public static StarCollectorDemoGame Instance;

    public List<StarCollectorDemoPeer> PeerList;

    private IFiber executionFiber;

    public void Startup()
    {
      // create a new execution fiber and start it
      executionFiber = new PoolFiber();
      executionFiber.Start();

      PeerList = new List<StarCollectorDemoPeer>();
    }
```

```
    public void Shutdown()
    {
      // dispose the execution fiber
      executionFiber.Dispose();
    }

    public void PeerJoined( StarCollectorDemoPeer peer )
    {
      // schedule peer to be added to PeerList on the main thread
      executionFiber.Enqueue( () =>
        {
          PeerList.Add( peer );
        } );
    }

    public void PeerLeft( StarCollectorDemoPeer peer )
    {
      // schedule peer to be removed from PeerList on the main
        thread
      executionFiber.Enqueue( () =>
      {
        PeerList.Remove( peer );
      } );
    }

    public void OnOperationRequest( StarCollectorDemoPeer sender,
      OperationRequest operationRequest, SendParameters
      sendParameters )
    {
      // schedule a message to be processed on the main thread
      executionFiber.Enqueue( () => { this.ProcessMessage( sender,
        operationRequest, sendParameters ); } );
    }

    public void ProcessMessage( StarCollectorDemoPeer sender,
      OperationRequest operationRequest, SendParameters
      sendParameters )
    {
      // process messages here
    }
  }
}
```

We now have convenient access to a list of peers currently connected to the server. Now, we have a framework in place, so let's start working on the actual game code.

The Actor class

I want all objects in the game to have a common base. While this isn't necessary, it often makes for better organization, and limits code reuse as common functionality can be defined in parent classes. So, let's create an `Actor` class for this. The `Actor` class will form the basis for Player objects, Stars, or whatever else we decide to add.

```
using Photon.SocketServer;

namespace StarCollectorDemo
{
  public class Actor
  {
    public PeerBase Owner; // the Peer that owns this actor, or
      NULL if actor is owned by server
    public long ActorID; // the ID of this actor instance
    public byte ActorType; // the type of this actor (player,
      star, etc)
    public float PosX; // the world X position of this actor
    public float PosY; // the world Y position of this actor
    public float Radius; // the collision radius of this actor
  }
}
```

We'll also create a `Star` class:

```
using Photon.SocketServer;
namespace StarCollectorDemo
{
  public class Star : Actor
  {
    public Star()
    {
      this.ActorType = 0; // star
      this.Radius = 0.25f; // radius, used to detect pickup
    }

    public bool DetectCollision( Actor other )
    {
      // calculate square distance between actors
      float sqrDist = ( ( this.PosX - other.PosX ) * ( this.PosX -
        other.PosX ) + ( this.PosY - other.PosY ) * ( this.PosY -
        other.PosY ) );

      // if the distance is less than the sum of the radii,
        collision occurs
```

```
        if( sqrDist <= ( this.Radius + other.Radius ) )
        {
          return true;
        }

        return false;
      }
    }
  }
```

Our `Star` class also detects collisions with other actors via the `DetectCollision` method. This is used to detect when a player walks over a `Star` class and picks it up.

Finally, the `Player` class. We're actually going to make our movement semi-server authoritative. So, a player provides a movement direction, and the server will set the velocity of the player. At regular intervals, the server will broadcast the absolute position and velocity of all player objects using the following code:

```
using Photon.SocketServer;

namespace StarCollectorDemo
{
  public class Player : Actor
  {
    public float VelocityX = 0f; // the X velocity of the player
    public float VelocityY = 0f; // the Y velocity of the player

    public int Score = 0; // the number of stars this player has
      collected

    public Player()
    {
      this.ActorType = 1; // player
      this.Radius = 0.5f; // radius, used to detect pickup
    }

    public void Simulate( float timestep )
    {
      this.PosX += this.VelocityX * timestep;
      this.PosY += this.VelocityY * timestep;
    }
  }
}
```

Sending an ID to a player

As before, we'll need to assign player IDs to our peers. Again, we'll just keep an incrementing static counter, and send the ID of a player to them when they connect. This becomes useful as we need a way to provide info about which peer owns a given player object.

```
using Photon.SocketServer;
using PhotonHostRuntimeInterfaces;

namespace StarCollectorDemo
{
  public class StarCollectorDemoPeer : PeerBase
  {
    private static long lastAssignedID = long.MinValue;
    private static object allocateIDLock = new object();

    public long PlayerID;

    public StarCollectorDemoPeer( IRpcProtocol protocol,
      IPhotonPeer unmanagedPeer )
      : base( protocol, unmanagedPeer )
    {
      lock( StarCollectorDemoGame.Instance )
      {
        StarCollectorDemoGame.Instance.PeerJoined( this );
      }

      lock( allocateIDLock )
      {
        PlayerID = lastAssignedID;
        lastAssignedID++;
      }

      //notify player of their ID
      EventData evt = new EventData();
      evt.Code = (byte)StarCollectorEventTypes.ReceivePlayerID;
      evt.Parameters = new System.Collections.Generic.Dictionary
        <byte, object>();
      evt.Parameters[ 0 ] = PlayerID;

      this.SendEvent( evt, new SendParameters() );
    }
```

```
    protected override void OnDisconnect( DisconnectReason
      reasonCode, string reasonDetail )
    {
      lock( StarCollectorDemoGame.Instance )
      {
        StarCollectorDemoGame.Instance.PeerLeft( this );
      }
    }
    protected override void OnOperationRequest( OperationRequest
      operationRequest, SendParameters sendParameters )
    {
      StarCollectorDemoGame.Instance.OnOperationRequest( this,
        operationRequest, sendParameters );
    }
  }
}
```

We'll also add an `enum` variable instance for event types:

```
namespace StarCollectorDemo
{
  public enum StarCollectorEventTypes : byte
  {
    ReceivePlayerID = 0,
  }
}
```

So now, when a player connects they receive player ID. This can be used to check, for example, which objects a player owns, or who sent a specific message (for instance move messages).

Keeping track of the game state

Now, we're going to add to our `Game` class a list of actors. We'll separate our `Stars` and `Players` for easier management, although in production games you'll likely want to unify your actor management (this way you can more easily extend the types of actors your game has).

First, we'll add some variables:

```
public List<Star> Stars = new List<Star>();
public List<Player> Players = new List<Player>();

private long lastAssignedActorID = long.MinValue;

private System.Random rand = new System.Random();
```

Next, we'll add a function to allocate an object ID for actors using the following code:

```
public long AllocateActorID()
{
    return lastAssignedActorID++;
}
```

We'll add a couple of methods to spawn objects—one for spawning stars, and the other for spawning players:

```
public void SpawnStar()
{
    // find a random position
    double x = rand.NextDouble();
    double y = rand.NextDouble();

    // map to the range -50, +50
    x -= 0.5f;
    x *= 100f; // 0.5 * 100 = 50
    y -= 0.5f;
    y *= 100f;

    Star star = new Star();
    star.PosX = (float)x;
    star.PosY = (float)y;

    star.ActorID = AllocateActorID();

    Stars.Add( star );
}
public void SpawnPlayer( StarCollectorDemoPeer peer )
{
    Player player = new Player();
    player.Owner = peer;
    player.ActorID = AllocateActorID();

    Players.Add( player );
}
```

We'll modify our `PeerJoined` and `PeerLeft` methods to create and destroy player objects:

```
public void PeerJoined( StarCollectorDemoPeer peer )
{
    // schedule peer to be added to PeerList on the main thread
    executionFiber.Enqueue( () =>
        {
            PeerList.Add( peer );
```

```
        SpawnPlayer( peer );
    } );
}


public void PeerLeft( StarCollectorDemoPeer peer )
{
  // schedule peer to be removed from PeerList on the main thread
  executionFiber.Enqueue( () =>
  {
    PeerList.Remove( peer );

    // remove player object belonging to this peer
    Players.RemoveAll( player => { return player.Owner == peer; }
      );
  } );
}
```

And finally, we'll add a Simulate function to simulate players and detect collisions between players and stars using the following code:

```
public void Simulate( float timeStep )
{
  // copy star collection so we can modify collection while
    iterating
  Star[] stars = Stars.ToArray();

  foreach( Player player in Players )
  {
    // simulate "physics"
    player.Simulate( timeStep );

    // compare player with each star
    foreach( Star star in stars )
    {
      if( star.DetectCollision( player ) )
      {
        // collision detected with star
      }
    }
  }
}
```

So, we're now keeping track of stars and players. Players are created when a peer joins, and removed when the peer leaves. In every game tick, players are simulated, and then compared against each star for collision.

There are a few things remaining. We still need to spawn new stars at the beginning of the round, destroy stars, and increment scores when they are picked up, and send events to clients when these occur so clients stay synchronized with the game state.

Spawning and picking up stars

First, we'll create a new InitRound method. This method will reset all players, and spawn hundred stars. Add this to your Game class:

```
public void InitRound()
{
  // reset players
  foreach( Player player in Players )
  {
    player.PosX = 0f;
    player.PosY = 0f;
    player.VelocityX = 0f;
    player.VelocityY = 0f;
    player.Score = 0;
  }

  // spawn new stars
  for( int i = 0; i < 100; i++ )
  {
    SpawnStar();
  }
}
```

And, we'll start by calling this in the Startup method of our game, so a round is started as soon as the server starts up.

```
public void Startup()
{
  // create a new execution fiber and start it
  executionFiber = new PoolFiber();
  executionFiber.Start();

  PeerList = new List<StarCollectorDemoPeer>();

  // start a new round
  InitRound();
}
```

We'll also handle the case of stars being picked up by players with a new function:

```
public void StarPickedUp( Star star, Player taker )
{
  Stars.Remove( star );

  taker.Score++;

  if( Stars.Count == 0 )
  {
    // the round is over!

    // restart round
    InitRound();
  }
}
```

And we'll call this when a collision is detected with a star:

```
public void Simulate( float timeStep )
{
  // copy star collection so we can modify collection while
    iterating
  Star[] stars = Stars.ToArray();

  foreach( Player player in Players )
  {
    // simulate "physics"
    player.Simulate( timeStep );

    // compare player with each star
    foreach( Star star in stars )
    {
      if( star.DetectCollision( player ) )
      {
        // collision detected with star
        StarPickedUp( star, player );
      }
    }
  }
}
```

Our server logic is almost complete. We still need to announce the winner, as well as broadcast important events to clients.

Broadcasting events

We're going to start broadcasting important gameplay events to players.

When a player joins, we first need to inform them of all available actors in the scene.

We'll add some event types for creating, destroying, and updating actors.

```
namespace StarCollectorDemo
{
  public enum StarCollectorEventTypes : byte
  {
    ReceivePlayerID = 0,
    CreateActor = 1,
    DestroyActor = 2,
    UpdateActor = 3
  }
}
```

We'll also add a new method to our Game class for broadcasting events to all connected peers:

```
public void BroadcastEvent( IEventData evt, SendParameters param )
{
  foreach( StarCollectorDemoPeer peer in PeerList )
  {
    peer.SendEvent( evt, param );
  }
}
```

Now, let's broadcast events for when players or stars are created. In our SpawnStar method:

```
public void SpawnStar()
{
  // find a random position
  double x = rand.NextDouble();
  double y = rand.NextDouble();
  // map to the range -50, +50
  x -= 0.5f;
  x *= 100f; // 0.5 * 100 = 50
  y -= 0.5f;
  y *= 100f;
  Star star = new Star();
  star.PosX = (float)x;
```

```
    star.PosY = (float)y;

    star.ActorID = AllocateActorID();

    Stars.Add( star );

    EventData evt = new EventData(
      (byte)StarCollectorEventTypes.CreateActor );
    evt.Parameters = new Dictionary<byte, object>();
    evt.Parameters[ 0 ] = star.ActorType;
    evt.Parameters[ 1 ] = star.ActorID;
    evt.Parameters[ 2 ] = star.PosX;
    evt.Parameters[ 3 ] = star.PosY;

    BroadcastEvent( evt, new SendParameters() );
}
```

When broadcasting a `CreateActor` event for Stars, we don't need to send info about owner ID because Stars are always owned by the server.

Our player `CreateActor` event looks much the same, but we'll also broadcast the player ID of the owner:

```
public void SpawnPlayer( StarCollectorDemoPeer peer )
{
  Player player = new Player();
  player.Owner = peer;
  player.ActorID = AllocateActorID();

  Players.Add( player );

  EventData evt = new EventData(
    (byte)StarCollectorEventTypes.CreateActor );
  evt.Parameters = new Dictionary<byte, object>();
  evt.Parameters[ 0 ] = player.ActorType;
  evt.Parameters[ 1 ] = player.ActorID;
  evt.Parameters[ 2 ] = player.PosX;
  evt.Parameters[ 3 ] = player.PosY;
  evt.Parameters[ 4 ] = peer.PlayerID;

  BroadcastEvent( evt, new SendParameters() );
}
```

When a player leaves, we'll need to broadcast a `DestroyActor` event:

```
public void PeerLeft( StarCollectorDemoPeer peer )
{
  // schedule peer to be removed from PeerList on the main thread
  executionFiber.Enqueue( () =>
  {
    PeerList.Remove( peer );
```

```
            // find the player object belonging to the peer
            Player player = Players.Find( actor => { return actor.Owner
              == peer; } );

            // broadcast DestroyActor event with player's actor ID
            EventData evt = new EventData(
              (byte)StarCollectorEventTypes.DestroyActor );
            evt.Parameters = new Dictionary<byte, object>();
            evt.Parameters[ 0 ] = player.ActorID;

            BroadcastEvent( evt, new SendParameters() );

            // remove from Players list
            Players.Remove( player );
        } );
}
```

Note that the `DestroyActor` event only needs to contain an Actor ID. Clients can look up at game object by using an Actor ID and destroy the game object.

And, we'll need to do the same when a Star is picked up:

```
public void StarPickedUp( Star star, Player taker )
{
  Stars.Remove( star );

  // broadcast DestroyActor event
  EventData evt = new EventData(
    (byte)StarCollectorEventTypes.DestroyActor );
  evt.Parameters = new Dictionary<byte, object>();
  evt.Parameters[ 0 ] = star.ActorID;

  BroadcastEvent( evt, new SendParameters() );

  taker.Score++;

  if( Stars.Count == 0 )
  {
    // the round is over!

    // restart round
    InitRound();
  }
}
```

We also need to make sure we send the current game state to new clients. We'll iterate through each player and star, sending the CreateActor events to the new peer (rather than broadcasting them).

```
public void PeerJoined( StarCollectorDemoPeer peer )
{
  // schedule peer to be added to PeerList on the main thread
  executionFiber.Enqueue( () =>
    {
      PeerList.Add( peer );

      // send player CreateActor events for all players and stars

      foreach( Player p in Players )
      {
        EventData evt = new EventData(
          (byte)StarCollectorEventTypes.CreateActor );
        evt.Parameters = new Dictionary<byte, object>();
        evt.Parameters[ 0 ] = p.ActorType;
        evt.Parameters[ 1 ] = p.ActorID;
        evt.Parameters[ 2 ] = p.PosX;
        evt.Parameters[ 3 ] = p.PosY;
        evt.Parameters[ 4 ] = ( p.Owner as StarCollectorDemoPeer
          ).PlayerID;

        peer.SendEvent( evt, new SendParameters() );
      }

      foreach( Star s in Stars )
      {
        EventData evt = new EventData(
          (byte)StarCollectorEventTypes.CreateActor );
        evt.Parameters = new Dictionary<byte, object>();
        evt.Parameters[ 0 ] = s.ActorType;
        evt.Parameters[ 1 ] = s.ActorID;
        evt.Parameters[ 2 ] = s.PosX;
        evt.Parameters[ 3 ] = s.PosY;

        peer.SendEvent( evt, new SendParameters() );
      }

      SpawnPlayer( peer );
    } );
}
```

We will also want to broadcast chat messages. So let's add a new event type for this:

```
namespace StarCollectorDemo
{
  public enum StarCollectorEventTypes : byte
  {
    ReceivePlayerID = 0,
    CreateActor = 1,
    DestroyActor = 2,
    UpdateActor = 3,
    ChatMessage = 4
  }
}
```

For now, we'll broadcast one thing: When the last star is picked up, we'll broadcast a chat message announcing the winner.

We'll be using LINQ to do this. We will order the players by Score, descending, and then pick the first player in the list (this is the player with the highest score). We display a chat message announcing the winner, before restarting the round.

```
public void StarPickedUp( Star star, Player taker )
{
  Stars.Remove( star );

  // broadcast DestroyActor event
  EventData evt = new EventData( (byte)StarCollectorEventTypes.
DestroyActor );
  evt.Parameters = new Dictionary<byte, object>();
  evt.Parameters[ 0 ] = star.ActorID;

  BroadcastEvent( evt, new SendParameters() );

  taker.Score++;

  if( Stars.Count == 0 )
  {
    // the round is over!

    // order players by score, pick the player with the highest score
    Player winner = ( from p in Players orderby taker.Score
      descending select p ).First();

    // broadcast a chat message
    EventData chatEvt = new EventData(
      (byte)StarCollectorEventTypes.ChatMessage );
```

```
        chatEvt.Parameters = new Dictionary<byte, object>();
        chatEvt.Parameters[0] = "Player " + ( winner.Owner as
           StarCollectorDemoPeer).PlayerID.ToString() + " wins the round
           with " + winner.Score + " stars!";

        BroadcastEvent( chatEvt, new SendParameters() );

        // restart round
        InitRound();
    }
}
```

There is one final event we need to broadcast. After every simulate tick, we'll broadcast move events for each player (our simulate will happen ten times per second). This is what the `UpdateActor` event code is for:

```
public void Simulate( float timeStep )
{
  // copy star collection so we can modify collection while iterating
  Star[] stars = Stars.ToArray();

  foreach( Player player in Players )
  {
    // simulate "physics"
    player.Simulate( timeStep );

    // broadcast move event
    EventData moveEvt = new EventData(
      (byte)StarCollectorEventTypes.UpdateActor );
    moveEvt.Parameters = new Dictionary<byte, object>();
    moveEvt.Parameters[ 0 ] = player.ActorID;
    moveEvt.Parameters[ 1 ] = player.PosX;
    moveEvt.Parameters[ 2 ] = player.PosY;

    BroadcastEvent( moveEvt, new SendParameters() );

    // compare player with each star
    foreach( Star star in stars )
    {
      if( star.DetectCollision( player ) )
      {
        // collision detected with star
        StarPickedUp( star, player );
      }
    }
  }
}
```

We also need to respond, to some kind of move request from the player. We'll add a new request code for this:

```
namespace StarCollectorDemo
{
  public enum StarCollectorRequestTypes : byte
  {
    MoveCommand = 0
  }
}
```

And when processing a request, if it's a move command from the player we'll set the player's velocity:

```
public void ProcessMessage( StarCollectorDemoPeer sender,
  OperationRequest operationRequest, SendParameters sendParameters )
{
  if( operationRequest.OperationCode ==
    (byte)StarCollectorRequestTypes.MoveCommand )
  {
    // move command from player
    long actorID = (long)operationRequest.Parameters[ 0 ];
    float velX = (float)operationRequest.Parameters[ 1 ];
    float velY = (float)operationRequest.Parameters[ 2 ];

    // find actor
    Player player = ( Players.Find( pl => { return pl.ActorID ==
actorID; } ) );

    // apply velocity
    player.VelocityX = velX;
    player.VelocityY = velY;
  }
}
```

Now, players can send a MoveCommand operation request to the server, which modifies the server-side player actor velocity.

Our game logic is now complete. There is one final thing to take care of before our server is fully functional, and that is starting up a game loop, which calls our Simulate method on a regular basis. Luckily we can take advantage of our execution fiber to schedule a repeating event:

```
public void Startup()
{
  // create a new execution fiber and start it
```

```
executionFiber = new PoolFiber();
executionFiber.Start();

PeerList = new List<StarCollectorDemoPeer>();

// start a new round
InitRound();

// schedule Simulate 10 times per second, or once every 100
  milliseconds
executionFiber.ScheduleOnInterval(
  delegate()
  {
    Simulate( 0.1f );
  }, 0, 100 );
}
```

And our server is now fully functional. All that remains is to connect to it from Unity and handle the various events from the server.

Connecting from Unity

The first thing we'll do is create a peer listener to connect to our server.

```
using UnityEngine;
using System.Collections;

using ExitGames.Client.Photon;

public class StarCollectorClient : MonoBehaviour,
  IPhotonPeerListener
{
  public static PhotonPeer Connection;
  public static bool Connected = false;
  public static long PlayerID;

  public string ServerIP = "127.0.0.1:5055";
  public string AppName = "StarCollectorDemo";

  void Start()
  {
    Debug.Log( "Connecting..." );
    Connection = new PhotonPeer( this, ConnectionProtocol.Udp );
    Connection.Connect( ServerIP, AppName );
```

```
      StartCoroutine( doService() );
    }
  void OnDestroy()
  {
    // explicitly disconnect if the client game object is destroyed
      if( Connected )
        Connection.Disconnect();
  }

    // update peer 20 times per second
    IEnumerator doService()
    {
      while( true )
      {
        Connection.Service();
        yield return new WaitForSeconds( 0.05f );
      }
    }
    #region IPhotonPeerListener Members
    public void DebugReturn( DebugLevel level, string message )
    {
      // log message to console
      Debug.Log( message );
    }
    public void OnEvent( EventData eventData )
    {
      //server raised an event
    }
    public void OnOperationResponse( OperationResponse
      operationResponse )
    {
      //server sent operation response
    }
    public void OnStatusChanged( StatusCode statusCode )
    {
      // log status change
      Debug.Log( "Status change: " + statusCode.ToString() );
      switch( statusCode )
      {
        case StatusCode.Connect:
          Debug.Log( "Connected, awaiting player ID..." );
          break;
        case StatusCode.Disconnect:
```

```
            case StatusCode.DisconnectByServer:
            case StatusCode.DisconnectByServerLogic:
            case StatusCode.DisconnectByServerUserLimit:
            case StatusCode.Exception:
            case StatusCode.ExceptionOnConnect:
            case StatusCode.SecurityExceptionOnConnect:
            case StatusCode.TimeoutDisconnect:
              StopAllCoroutines();
              Connected = false;
              break;
        }
    }

    #endregion
}
```

Firstly, startup connects to our server and begins servicing the peer 20 times per second. If any exceptions, it disconnects, or timeouts occur, it stops servicing the peer and sets connected to false. If the peer reports that, it has connected to our application, we print a debug message (stating that our application is waiting for the player ID, after which it will receive the game state).

Before we continue, copy the enum variable instances we defined on the server (StarCollectorRequestTypes and StarCollectorEventTypes) to your Unity project.

The first thing we'll do is receive the player ID and store it in a static long variable is as follows:

```
public void OnEvent( EventData eventData )
{
  //server raised an event
  switch( (StarCollectorEventTypes)eventData.Code )
  {
    // store player ID
    case StarCollectorEventTypes.ReceivePlayerID:
      long playerId = (long)eventData.Parameters[ 0 ];
      PlayerID = playerId;
      break;
  }
}
```

Now, when the client connects, it will store its player ID, which is used to check which player actor it owns.

Creating/destroying actors

Next, we'll handle `CreateActor`/`DestroyActor` events by spawning and deleting game objects. The first thing we'll do is create some scripts, one to store the actor ID and the other to store the owner ID. Stars will only need the actor ID component, but players will need both.

Our actor ID component looks like this:

```
using UnityEngine;
using System.Collections;
using System.Collections.Generic;

public class GameActor : MonoBehaviour
{
  public static Dictionary<long, GameActor> Actors = new
Dictionary<long, GameActor>();

  public long ActorID;

  void SetActorID( long actorID )
  {
    this.ActorID = actorID;
    Actors.Add( this.ActorID, this );
  }

  public void Destruct()
  {
    Actors.Remove( this.ActorID );
    Destroy( gameObject );
  }
}
```

When we spawn an actor, we need to call `SetActorID` immediately. This causes the object to be stored in a `Dictionary` object. The `Dictionary` object allows us to easily look up at actors by ID. The `Destruct` method is mostly for convenience, which handles cleaning up the `Dictionary` object entry and destroying the actual game object.

We'll also make an `OwnerID` component using following code:

```
using UnityEngine;
using System.Collections;

public class OwnerInfo : MonoBehaviour
{
```

```
    public long OwnerID;

    public bool IsMine
    {
      get
      {
        return OwnerID == StarCollectorClient.PlayerID;
      }
    }

    void SetOwnerID( long ownerID )
    {
      this.OwnerID = ownerID;
    }
}
```

The most important part of this script is checking whether or not the object belongs to the local client, based on the OwnerID.

Now that we've created the necessary components, let's make some prefabs for the players and stars.

First, the Player prefab. Create a Cube, and attach the GameActor and OwnerInfo scripts. Save this as a prefab in your project. For the Star, create a Cube, scale it down to *0.5 x 0.5 x 0.5*, and attach the GameActor component. Save this as a prefab, too.

Now, we'll modify our Client class to handle the Create and Destroy events.

First, we'll add some prefab references to the top of our script:

```
public class StarCollectorClient : MonoBehaviour, IPhotonPeerListener
{
  public static PhotonPeer Connection;
  public static bool Connected = false;
  public static long PlayerID;

  public string ServerIP = "127.0.0.1:5055";
  public string AppName = "StarCollectorDemo";

  public GameObject PlayerPrefab;
  public GameObject StarPrefab;

  // [...]
```

And, handle the appropriate events in our `OnEvent` method:

```
public void OnEvent( EventData eventData )
{
  //server raised an event
  switch( (StarCollectorEventTypes)eventData.Code )
  {
    // store player ID
    case StarCollectorEventTypes.ReceivePlayerID:
      long playerId = (long)eventData.Parameters[ 0 ];
      PlayerID = playerId;
      Debug.Log( "Received player ID, awaiting game state..." );
      break;
    // spawn actor
    case StarCollectorEventTypes.CreateActor:
      byte actorType = (byte)eventData.Parameters[ 0 ];
      long actorID = (long)eventData.Parameters[ 1 ];
      float posX = (float)eventData.Parameters[ 2 ];
      float posY = (float)eventData.Parameters[ 3 ];
      GameObject actor = null;
      switch( actorType )
      {
        // Star
        case 0:
          actor = (GameObject)Instantiate( StarPrefab, new Vector3(
            posX, 0f, posY ), Quaternion.identity );
          break;
        // Player
        case 1:
          long ownerID = (long)eventData.Parameters[ 4 ];
          actor = (GameObject)Instantiate( PlayerPrefab, new Vector3
            ( posX, 0f, posY ), Quaternion.identity );
          actor.SendMessage( "SetOwnerID", ownerID );
          break;
      }
      actor.SendMessage( "SetActorID", actorID );
      break;
    // destroy actor
    case StarCollectorEventTypes.DestroyActor:
      GameActor destroyActor = GameActor.Actors[
        (long)eventData.Parameters[ 0 ] ];
      if( destroyActor != null )
        destroyActor.Destruct();
      break;
  }
}
```

Place your client script on an empty game object (if you haven't already) and assign the `Player` and `Star` prefabs to the appropriate slots. If you run the server and connect from Unity, you will now see a field of randomly placed "stars" and a single "player" in the middle of the field. We're almost there, just a few things left to implement: Adding controls to the player object, receiving movement updates, and displaying chat messages.

Controlling the player

The first thing we'll do, is create a `Player` script. This script will allow us to control the `Player` object if it belongs to us. We will use the following code for performing this:

```
using UnityEngine;
using System.Collections;
using System.Collections.Generic;

public class Player : MonoBehaviour
{
  public float MoveSpeed = 5f;

  private OwnerInfo ownerInfo;
  private GameActor actorInfo;
  private bool isMine = false;

  private Vector3 lastReceivedMove;

  private float timeOfLastMoveCmd = 0f;

  void Start()
  {
    timeOfLastMoveCmd = Time.time;

    lastReceivedMove = transform.position;

    ownerInfo = GetComponent<OwnerInfo>();
    actorInfo = GetComponent<GameActor>();
    isMine = ( ownerInfo.OwnerID == StarCollectorClient.PlayerID );
  }

  void Update()
  {
    if( isMine )
    {
```

```
        // get movement direction
        float mX = Input.GetAxis( "Horizontal" ) * MoveSpeed;
        float mY = Input.GetAxis( "Vertical" ) * MoveSpeed;

        if( Time.time >= timeOfLastMoveCmd + 0.1f )
        {
            timeOfLastMoveCmd = Time.time;

            // send move command to server every 0.1 seconds
            Dictionary<byte, object> moveParams = new Dictionary<byte,
object>();
            moveParams[ 0 ] = actorInfo.ActorID;
            moveParams[ 1 ] = mX;
            moveParams[ 2 ] = mY;
            StarCollectorClient.Connection.OpCustom( (byte)
StarCollectorRequestTypes.MoveCommand, moveParams, false );
        }
    }

    // lerp toward last received position
    transform.position = Vector3.Lerp( transform.position,
        lastReceivedMove, Time.deltaTime * 20f );
    }

    void UpdatePosition( Vector3 newPos )
    {
        lastReceivedMove = newPos;
    }
}
```

This script goes on our `Player` prefab. It first grabs a reference to the `GameActor` component, and the `OwnerInfo` component. It then checks and stores whether the actor belongs to the local player by comparing the `OwnerID` with the local `PlayerID`.

If the actor does belong to the player, it proceeds to process input commands. Every 0.1 seconds (ten times per second), it sends a `Move` command to the server, which tells the server to update the velocity of the given actor.

Additionally, it keeps track of a "last received position". When we receive move updates from the server, we'll call the `UpdatePosition` method on the appropriate actor. This will cause the actor to lerp toward that position.

Next, let's start receiving move commands from the server. We'll find the appropriate actor and call `SendMessage` to update it's position. In the `switch` statement of the `OnEvent` method of our `StarCollectorClient`, we'll add this case:

```
// update actor
case StarCollectorEventTypes.UpdateActor:
  GameActor updateActor = GameActor.Actors[
    (long)eventData.Parameters[ 0 ] ];
  float newPosX = (float)eventData.Parameters[ 1 ];
  float newPosY = (float)eventData.Parameters[ 2 ];
  updateActor.SendMessage( "UpdatePosition", new Vector3(
    newPosX, 0f, newPosY ), SendMessageOptions.
    DontRequireReceiver );
  break;
```

We're also going to display chat messages. For this example, we'll debug log them (a real game would display them in the GUI, such as in a chatbox). So we'll add another case for chat messages:

```
// log chat messages
case StarCollectorEventTypes.ChatMessage:
  Debug.Log( (string)eventData.Parameters[ 0 ] );
  break;
```

There is one final thing we should do. In our main scene, we'll move the camera to give an overhead view of the game world. Set the camera to **Orthographic**, move it to (0,100,0), and set the **Orthographic Size** to 51. This should give the camera enough room to see all of the stars (50 would be enough, but the extra 1 adds a slight border, which makes it easier to see stars on the edge).

Now, make sure your server is running, and start up the main scene. You should see the playing field populated with hundred small cubes, and a single larger cube in the center. You should be able to control your cube with the arrow keys, and collect stars by moving over them. When all stars are collected, your cube moves back to the center, all stars are re-spawned, and the console displays your `PlayerID` as the winner of the game (for example, `"Player -9223372036854775808 is the winner with 100 stars!"`)

Summary

In this chapter, we have learned what makes Photon Server different from middleware, such as Unity Networking or Photon Unity Networking. We learned how to connect to a Photon Server, send operation requests, and receive events or operation responses. We also learned how to make a custom server application that receives these requests and sends back responses, or broadcasts events.

We then applied these concepts to create a simple star collector game, where players race to collect as many "stars" as possible, and the player with the most stars, after all stars are collected wins the game.

In the next chapter, we will cover another dedicated server technology known as Player.IO.

4
Player.IO – Bot Wars

In the last chapter, we have covered our first dedicated server technology, Photon Server. In this chapter, we will be covering another dedicated server technology known as Player.IO.

Just like Photon Server, Player.IO runs dedicated server code, where players connect to the server and send messages, and the server processes game logic. Player.IO also includes a variety of other features such as login/account systems, databases, leaderboards, and so on. Additionally, it is similar to Photon Cloud in that servers are hosted by the service, and cannot be self-hosted.

In this chapter we will cover the following topics:

- What makes Player.IO different from Photon Server
- Setting up a development server instance
- Setting up the Unity client SDK
- Connecting to Player.IO, joining rooms, and sending/receiving messages
- Loading and saving data via BigDB
- Generating instant object IDs client-side
- Creating a simple multiplayer RTS prototype

Let's dive in.

Player.IO versus the Photon Server

Player.IO does a number of things differently from Photon Server. One of the biggest differences is that Player.IO is cloud-hosted. That is, your game code runs on a cluster of shared servers (whereas Photon requires you to host your own server), and it is also possible to rent dedicated clusters in this cloud. Additionally, Player.IO is room-based. Upon connecting to Player.IO, you specify a room to connect to, and players are segregated into different rooms. For instance, in an MMO you might have different "rooms" for regions in the world. Without a dedicated cluster, rooms are limited to 45 players. If you rent a dedicated cluster, there is no limit.

One final, big difference in Player.IO: as Player.IO was originally designed for Flash applications, and Flash does not support UDP, Player.IO supports TCP only. Additionally, Player.IO has a strict limit on message processing, and too many messages can result in disconnects.

Other than that, most concepts learned with Photon will apply to Player.IO, although the specifics may be different. With that aside, let's set up a development server for testing.

Getting and setting up a development server

First, you'll need to sign up for a Player.IO developer account here: `https://playerio.com/register`.

You will need to create a new game from the dashboard, so follow the **Go** to admin panel link after logging in and click on the **Create New Game** button. Copy the game ID for later, as we'll need it for connecting.

Next, download the developer package, which contains Flash and Unity client SDKs, and the development server: `https://playerio.com/download/`.

After downloading and unzipping this, navigate to the Flash folder and copy the `NewGame` folder. Paste this wherever you like (I usually paste it into the same directory) and rename it, then delete the `Flash` folder inside. Now, you can open the SLN file to begin developing.

The first time you run the server (by pressing *F5* with the solution open) it will ask for your credentials. Supply your developer username and password and log in. username and password are stored on a per-server basis. If you ever need to log out (for instance, before passing on server code to a third-party), there is a log out button at the top-right corner of the server application.

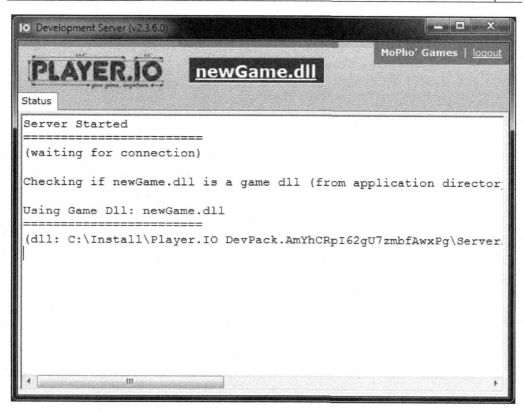

Now, the server is ready for developing.

Setting up the Unity client SDK

To use the Unity client SDK, navigate to the Unity3D folder and copy the
PlayerIOUnity3DClient DLL and XML file. Paste these into a Plugins folder in
your Unity project.

Now, the Unity project is ready.

Connecting to Player.IO

The first thing we will do is connect to Player.IO. Note that connecting to Player.IO
does not involve actually connecting to our development server. Essentially,
our client connects to the Player.IO cloud service, and then joins a room in the
chosen cluster.

By default, Player.IO connects to the public cluster, but you can tell the client library to connect to the "development cluster" instead, which is your local server.

```csharp
using UnityEngine;
using System.Collections;

using PlayerIOClient;

public class ConnectToPlayerIO : MonoBehaviour
{
  Client client;

  void Start()
  {
    PlayerIO.UnityInit( this );

    // We connect to Player.IO here. Parameters are:
    // - The ID you copied earlier
    // - The connection type to use. "public" specifies the
    //   "public" connection. It's possible to have different
    //   connection types with different permissions, but on a Free
    //   account we only have access to "public".
    // - The ID you wish to give the player, usually screen name
    // - The auth token. You can make a connection type require
    //   authentication, and if this connection is used you pass an
    //   auth value generated from the user ID. Don't worry about
    //   this for now, just pass null. For information see:
    // http://playerio.com/documentation/connections
    // - The "partner" to use. Third parties can sign up with
    //   Player.IO to be "partners", and can negotiate deals with
    //   developers via the PartnerPay service. Don't worry about
    //   this for now, just pass null. For more information see:
    // http://playerio.com/documentation/partnerpay
    PlayerIO.Connect( "YourGameIDHere", "public",
      "YourUserIDHere", null, null,,
    delegate( Client c )
    {
      // connected successfully
      client = c;
      Debug.Log( "Connected" );
    },
    delegate( PlayerIOError error )
    {
```

```
        // did not connect successfully
        Debug.Log( error.Message );
      } );
    }
  }
```

Nearly all calls made to Player.IO, which are expected to return a result are done via delegates. Usually, this involves a success and a failure delegate. In this case, on success we get a client, which can be used to make calls to Player.IO services.

Once we have a client, we can make calls to the Multiplayer service. Before we do that, we'll tell the client to connect to our local development server for testing.

```
using UnityEngine;
using System.Collections;

using PlayerIOClient;

public class ConnectToPlayerIO : MonoBehaviour
{
  public bool UseDevServer = true;

  Client client;

  void Start()
  {
    PlayerIO.UnityInit( this );

    PlayerIO.Connect( "YourGameIDHere", "public",
      "YourUserIDHere", null, null,
    delegate( Client c )
    {
      // connected successfully
      client = c;
      Debug.Log( "Connected" );

      // if we're using the dev server, connect to the local IP
      // Note that the development server uses port 8184, this cannot
        be changed.
      if( UseDevServer )
      {
        client.Multiplayer.DevelopmentServer = new ServerEndpoint(
          "127.0.0.1", 8184 );
      }
    },
```

```
        delegate( PlayerIOError error )
        {
          // did not connect successfully
          Debug.Log( error.Message );
        } );
    }
  }
```

Now, when we go to connect to a game, our client will use the local server if `UseDevServer` is enabled.

Getting a list of rooms

Now that we're connected to Player.IO, and to our local server, we can get a list of rooms.

```
using UnityEngine;
using System.Collections;

using PlayerIOClient;

public class ConnectToPlayerIO : MonoBehaviour
{
  public bool UseDevServer = true;

  Client client;

  void Start()
  {
    PlayerIO.UnityInit( this );

    PlayerIO.Connect( "YourGameIDHere", "public",
      "YourUserIDHere", null, null,
    delegate( Client c )
    {
      // connected successfully
      client = c;
      Debug.Log( "Connected" );

      // if we're using the dev server, connect to the local IP
      if( UseDevServer )
      {
        client.Multiplayer.DevelopmentServer = new ServerEndpoint(
          "127.0.0.1", 8184 );
```

```
        GetRoomList();
      }
    },
    delegate( PlayerIOError error )
    {
      // did not connect successfully
      Debug.Log( error.Message );
    } );
  }

  void GetRoomList()
  {
    // get a list of all rooms with the given room type and search
      criteria (null = all rooms)
    client.Multiplayer.ListRooms( "SomeRoomType", null, 0, 0,
      delegate( RoomInfo[] rooms )
      {
        Debug.Log( "Found rooms: " + rooms.Length );
      },
      delegate( PlayerIOError error )
      {
        Debug.Log( error.Message );
      } );
  }
}
```

This code gets a list of all rooms, and displays the number of available rooms.

The first parameter to ListRooms is the room type. On your Player.IO server, you create a class for each room type. For instance, an FPS might have classes for Deathmatch, TeamDeathmatch, CaptureTheFlag, and so on. Each of these has a room type name assigned to it, and from the client we can query for the type of room we want to join.

The second parameter is a dictionary of search criteria, where each property must match between the search and the room. When a room is created on the server, it can be assigned a dictionary of room properties. For instance, in the same hypothetical FPS you might have room properties for player limit, time limit, friendly fire, map, and so on. The client would allow players to search for rooms matching specific criteria (for instance, only rooms where friendly fire is disabled) by providing a dictionary to the ListRooms function. Passing null disables the search criteria (so all rooms are returned).

The next two parameters are room count and result offset. Some games might implement a paged lobby, so the lobby might display 10 games at a time, and players hit next and previous buttons to navigate the pages. In that case, room count would be 10 and page offset would be which page the player is on, 0 for the first page, incrementing by 10 for each page. We'll use 0 for room count (return as many rooms as possible), and 0 for offset.

Before you run this, you will need to ensure your development server is running (open the solution and press *F5*).

If you run this code, you'll see it connect, and then list the number of room open (currently none).

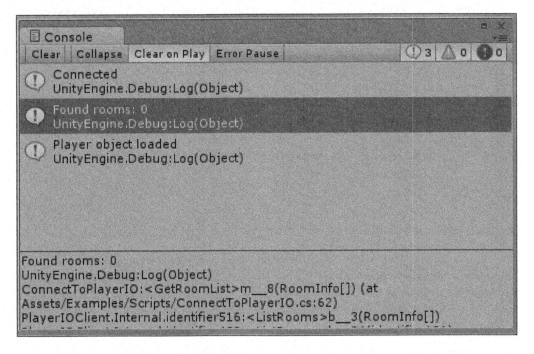

Connecting to rooms

After you have a list of rooms, you can connect to a room via the JoinRoom method. The JoinRoom method takes the name of the room, and can optionally take a dictionary of "join data", which is supplied to the room on connect. This join data can be used for a number of things (for example, supplying the username, if a room is password protected this might contain password, and so on).

Let's store the returned rooms and iterate them in OnGUI.

First, we'll add some variables, which are as follows:

```
Connection roomConnection;
private RoomInfo[] rooms = null;
```

Next, we'll modify our `GetRoomList` function:

```
void GetRoomList()
{
  // get a list of all rooms with the given room type and search
    criteria (null = all rooms)
  client.Multiplayer.ListRooms( "SomeRoomType", null, 0, 0,
    delegate( RoomInfo[] rooms )
    {
      Debug.Log( "Found rooms: " + rooms.Length );
      this.rooms = rooms;
    },
    delegate( PlayerIOError error )
    {
      Debug.Log( error.Message );
    } );
}
```

And finally, we'll iterate and display these in OnGUI. We can also take the opportunity to disconnect from whatever room we're in when the game client is closed. This is not strictly necessary, but good practice.

```
void OnGUI()
{
  // no room list yet - abort
  if( rooms == null )
    return;

  // iterate rooms in room list
  foreach( RoomInfo room in rooms )
  {
    // click button to join room
    if( GUILayout.Button( room.Id, GUILayout.Width( 200f ) ) )
    {
      client.Multiplayer.JoinRoom( room.Id, null,
        delegate( Connection connection )
        {
          Debug.Log( "Connected to room!" );
          // store room connection so we can send/receive messages
          roomConnection = connection;
        },
```

```
          delegate( PlayerIOError error )
          {
            Debug.Log( error.Message );
          } );
      }
    }
}

void OnApplicationQuit()
{
  // if the application quits, disconnect from whatever room we're
    connected to. Not strictly necessary, but good practice.
  if( roomConnection != null )
    roomConnection.Disconnect();
}
```

When you connect to a room, you get a connection object. This object is used to interact with the room, by sending and receiving messages. You can call the Send method to send a message, and you can register message handlers to receive messages.

Creating rooms

To create a room, there are two methods you can call: CreateRoom, and CreateJoinRoom. The CreateRoom method takes the desired room name (or null if you want a random room name), and room parameters (a dictionary of room properties, such as time limit, map, password, and so on). The CreateJoinRoom method takes both the properties of CreateRoom, and the properties of JoinRoom, as it will either join the room if it exists or create a new one.

One thing to note is that CreateRoom will not automatically establish a connection. It simply returns a string of the room ID on success, and then this is used to connect via JoinRoom.

```
void OnGUI()
{
  if( roomConnection != null )
    return;

  if( GUILayout.Button( "Create Room", GUILayout.Width( 200f ) ) )
  {
    // "MyCode" is the default room type provided with the Serverside
      Code solution
    client.Multiplayer.CreateRoom( null, "MyCode", true, null,
```

```
      delegate( string roomID )
      {
        Debug.Log( "Room created" );
        client.Multiplayer.JoinRoom( roomID, null,
        delegate( Connection connection )
        {

Debug.Log( "Connected to room!" );
roomConnection = connection;
        },
        delegate( PlayerIOError error )
        {
          Debug.Log( error.Message );
        } );
      },
      delegate( PlayerIOError error )
      {
        Debug.Log( error.Message );
      } );
  }

  if( rooms == null )
    return;

  foreach( RoomInfo room in rooms )
  {
    if( GUILayout.Button( room.Id, GUILayout.Width( 200f ) ) )
    {
      client.Multiplayer.JoinRoom( room.Id, null,
        delegate( Connection connection )
        {
          Debug.Log( "Connected to room!" );
          roomConnection = connection;
        },
        delegate( PlayerIOError error )
        {
          Debug.Log( error.Message );
        } );
    }
  }
}
```

So, we first attempt to create a room. If that succeeds, we then establish a connection to that room (and store the resulting connection in roomConnection).

Random matchmaking

It's also possible to employ a form of random matchmaking. That is, by supplying the special room ID "$service-room$" to CreateJoinRoom, you will connect the user to so called "Service Rooms". A service room is a room with a randomly created ID, and a new room will only be created when the existing service rooms are all filled up to 75 percent (this gives some leeway to move users between rooms). By using CreateJoinRoom, the client will create a room if it doesn't exist, or join the existing one if it does.

```
void OnGUI()
{
  if( roomConnection != null )
    return;

  if( GUILayout.Button( "Join Random", GUILayout.Width( 200f ) ) )
  {
    client.Multiplayer.CreateJoinRoom( "$service-room$", "MyCode",
      true, null, null,
      delegate( Connection connection )
      {
        Debug.Log( "Joining room" );
        roomConnection = connection;
      },
      delegate( PlayerIOError error )
      {
        Debug.Log( error.Message );
      } );
  }

  if( GUILayout.Button( "Create Room", GUILayout.Width( 200f ) ) )
  {
    client.Multiplayer.CreateRoom( null, "MyCode", true, null,
      delegate( string roomID )
      {
        Debug.Log( "Room created" );
        client.Multiplayer.JoinRoom( roomID, null,
          delegate( Connection connection )
          {
            Debug.Log( "Connected to room!" );
            roomConnection = connection;
          },
          delegate( PlayerIOError error )
          {
```

```
          Debug.Log( error.Message );
        } );
    },
    delegate( PlayerIOError error )
    {
      Debug.Log( error.Message );
    } );
}

if( rooms == null )
  return;

foreach( RoomInfo room in rooms )
{
  if( GUILayout.Button( room.Id, GUILayout.Width( 200f ) ) )
  {
    client.Multiplayer.JoinRoom( room.Id, null,
      delegate( Connection connection )
      {
        Debug.Log( "Connected to room!" );
        roomConnection = connection;
      },
      delegate( PlayerIOError error )
      {
        Debug.Log( error.Message );
      } );
  }
 }
}
```

Sending/receiving messages

Once connected to a room, we have a connection that can be used to send and
receive messages. Let's register event handlers for receiving messages, as well as
disconnections.

First, we'll add methods to handle these events:

```
// called when we've disconnected from the room
void OnDisconnect( object sender, string message )
{
  Debug.Log( "Disconnected from room" );
}
```

```
// called when a message is received
void OnMessage( object sender, Message e )
{
}
```

Then we'll modify our OnGUI method to hook up these event handlers upon connection:

```
void OnGUI()
{
  if( roomConnection != null )
    return;

  if( GUILayout.Button( "Join Random", GUILayout.Width( 200f ) ) )
  {
    client.Multiplayer.CreateJoinRoom( "$service-room$", "MyCode",
      true, null, null,
      delegate( Connection connection )
      {
        Debug.Log( "Joining room" );
        roomConnection = connection;
        roomConnection.OnMessage += new
          MessageReceivedEventHandler( OnMessage );
        roomConnection.OnDisconnect += new DisconnectEventHandler
          ( OnDisconnect );
      },
      delegate( PlayerIOError error )
      {
        Debug.Log( error.Message );
      } );
  }

  if( GUILayout.Button( "Create Room", GUILayout.Width( 200f ) ) )
  {
    client.Multiplayer.CreateRoom( null, "MyCode", true, null,
      delegate( string roomID )
      {
        Debug.Log( "Room created" );
        client.Multiplayer.JoinRoom( roomID, null,
        delegate( Connection connection )
        {
        Debug.Log( "Connected to room!" );
        roomConnection = connection;
        roomConnection.OnMessage += new
          MessageReceivedEventHandler( OnMessage );
```

```
      roomConnection.OnDisconnect += new DisconnectEventHandler
        ( OnDisconnect );
      },
      delegate( PlayerIOError error )
      {
        Debug.Log( error.Message );
      } );
    },
    delegate( PlayerIOError error )
    {
      Debug.Log( error.Message );
    } );
}

if( rooms == null )
  return;

foreach( RoomInfo room in rooms )
{
  if( GUILayout.Button( room.Id, GUILayout.Width( 200f ) ) )
  {
    client.Multiplayer.JoinRoom( room.Id, null,
      delegate( Connection connection )
      {
      Debug.Log( "Connected to room!" );
      roomConnection = connection;
      roomConnection.OnMessage += new
        MessageReceivedEventHandler( OnMessage );
      roomConnection.OnDisconnect += new DisconnectEventHandler
        ( OnDisconnect );
      },
      delegate( PlayerIOError error )
      {
        Debug.Log( error.Message );
      } );
  }
 }
}
```

When the room sends a message to the client, the OnMessage function will be called. If the client is disconnected from the room, the OnDisconnect function will be called.

To send messages, we simply call the `Send` method on the `Connection` object. This method can either take a `Message` object, or a string Message Type and parameter list. Usually it's easier to simply provide the type and parameter list, but you can also construct a Message via `Message.Create`, which takes the same type and parameter list and you can also add parameters via the `Add` method (for instance, allow objects to serialize their info by giving them the `Message` object and allowing them to add parameters).

So, at the top of our GUI function, we could add this to allow the user to send a test message while they're in a room:

```
if( roomConnection != null )
{
  if( GUILayout.Button( "Send Message", GUILayout.Width( 200f ) ) )
  {
    roomConnection.Send( "TestMessage", "Hello, world!" );
  }
  return;
}
```

The first parameter is message type, used to identify what kind of message it is (for instance, you might have a "move" message type, a "chat" message type, and so on). All other parameters are values added to the message payload (so, for instance a move message might contain X, Y, and Z position values, a chat message would have a single string message, and so on).

Server-side code

The Server code handles things a bit differently. You have a single function for processing messages from players (`GotMessage`); and can send a message to players either by calling `BroadcastMessage` (which broadcasts a message to all players), or by calling `Send` on a specific player (which sends to that player only). Note that Player.IO servers are multithreaded, so keep this in mind while writing code to ensure thread safety. The Client API is not multithreaded, however.

In the included server code, the default GotMessage function looks like this:

```
// This method is called when a player sends a message into the server
code
public override void GotMessage( Player player, Message message )
{
  switch( message.Type )
  {
    // This is how you would set a players name when they send in
       their name in a
```

```
    // "MyNameIs" message
    case "MyNameIs":
      player.Name = message.GetString( 0 );
      break;
  }
}
```

If you wanted to handle a specific message type, you would likely use cases in a switch-case for each type of message (as shown earlier). So, you might respond to the `TestMessage` type message like this:

```
// This method is called when a player sends a message into the server
code
public override void GotMessage( Player player, Message message )
{
  switch( message.Type )
  {
    // This is how you would set a players name when they send in
       their name in a
    // "MyNameIs" message
    case "MyNameIs":
      player.Name = message.GetString( 0 );
      break;
    case "TestMessage":
      player.Send( "TestResponse", message.GetString( 0 ) );
      break;
  }
}
```

When the player sends a `TestMessage` type message, the server responds with a `TestResponse` type message, containing the first string value in the `TestMessage` type message sent by the player.

Working with BigDB

Player.IO provides a database service known as BigDB. The objects can be saved to BigDB and loaded from BigDB, and there is also a concept of "ownership" of a database entry (for instance, you can configure databases so that players are only allowed to modify their own DB entries).

Both the server and the client can access BigDB. Note that development servers have the same permissions as the player—be aware of this, as restricting player permissions will also restrict developer permissions.

Note that BigDB is stored on Player.IO servers, not the local development server. The data can be viewed from the admin panel on the website. This data is stored per-game (for instance, so you cannot access the data for other games). Also be aware that no data is encrypted in Player.IO, so for instance storing passwords in plain text is not advised, just as with most conventional database systems.

BigDB also has a built-in player object's table. This is used to save data belonging to a player, and you can retrieve your player object using the `LoadMyPlayerObject` function:

```
DatabaseObject playerObj;

void Start()
{
  PlayerIO.UnityInit( this );

  PlayerIO.Connect( "YourGameIDHere", "public", "YourUserIDHere",
    null, null,
  delegate( Client c )
  {
    // connected successfully
    client = c;
    Debug.Log( "Connected" );

    // load the player object
    client.BigDB.LoadMyPlayerObject(
    delegate( DatabaseObject obj )
    {
      playerObj = obj;

      Debug.Log( "Player object loaded" );
    },
    delegate( PlayerIOError error )
    {
      Debug.Log( error.Message );
    } );

    // if we're using the dev server, connect to the local IP
    if( UseDevServer )
    {
```

```
        client.Multiplayer.DevelopmentServer = new ServerEndpoint
          ( "127.0.0.1", 8184 );

        GetRoomList();
      }
    },
    delegate( PlayerIOError error )
    {
      // did not connect successfully
      Debug.Log( error.Message );
    } );
}
```

This gives you a `DatabaseObject` instance. With a `DatabaseObject` instance you can set properties using the `Set` method, supplying a key and a value. The value can be one of the following types:

- Boolean
- Byte array
- Double
- Float
- Integer
- Long
- Unsigned Integer
- System.DateTime
- DatabaseObject
- DatabaseArray

 Keep in mind that database objects are limited to 500 kb in size.

The `DatabaseArrays` instances are similar to `DatabaseObjects`, except that they hold data in sequential indices rather than string keys. It's also possible to nest `DatabaseObjects` and `DatabaseArrays`, so for instance on your player object you could have a database array, which holds an array of items your player owns as `DatabaseObjects`.

Saving a `DatabaseObject` instance looks like this:

```
if( GUILayout.Button( "Save Test Player Object", GUILayout.Width
  ( 200f ) ) )
{
  playerObj.Set( "TestProperty", "someValue" );
  playerObj.Save(
  delegate()
  {
    Debug.Log( "Player object saved" );
  },
  delegate( PlayerIOError error )
  {
    Debug.Log( error.Message );
  } );
}
```

Besides `LoadMyPlayerObject`, you can also use several other methods such as `Load`, `LoadOrCreate` (which creates the object if it doesn't exist), `LoadKeys` (to load several at once), `LoadKeysOrCreate`, and `LoadRange` (which allows you to use an "index" to get a list of database objects, for instance you could use this to implement leaderboards by creating an index for scores).

For more information, please read the documentation on BigDB: `http://playerio.com/features/bigdb/`.

Creating a simple RTS prototype

Using the knowledge we've gained about Player.IO and applying the concepts from the previous chapter, we're going to create a simple RTS style game.

The player will own five bots. Each of these bots can be commanded to move, or attack another bot. The number of bots killed and lost will be recorded (and persisted to the database for a leaderboard).

Upon losing all five bots the player is kicked out of the game to the main menu.

Server-side code

We'll start by modifying the server code as follows:

```
using System;
using System.Collections.Generic;
using System.Text;
using System.Collections;
```

```
using PlayerIO.GameLibrary;
using System.Drawing;

namespace BotWarsGame
{
  public class Player : BasePlayer
  {
    public string Name;
  }

  // This attribute is used to identify the room type
  // When starting a room, you can specify room type - it
    corresponds to this value.
  // Note that the Game class is the base class for room code - it
    takes a Type which is the type to use for Players
  [RoomType( "GameRoom" )]
  public class GameCode : Game<Player>
  {
    // This method is called when an instance of your the game is
      created
    public override void GameStarted()
    {
    }

    // This method is called when the last player leaves the room,
      and it's closed down.
    public override void GameClosed()
    {
    }

    // This method is called whenever a player joins the game
    public override void UserJoined( Player player )
    {
      player.Name = player.JoinData[ "Name" ];

      // send the player their own ID
      player.Send( "SetID", player.Id );

      // inform everyone that this user has joined
      Broadcast( "UserJoined", player.Id, player.Name );

      // inform the user of everyone else in the room,
      foreach( Player p in Players )
      {
        if( p == player )
```

```
            continue;

          player.Send( "UserJoined", player.Id, player.Name );
        }
    }

    // This method is called when a player leaves the game
    public override void UserLeft( Player player )
    {
      Broadcast( "UserLeft", player.Id );
    }

    // This method is called when a player sends a message into
      the server code
    public override void GotMessage( Player player, Message
      message )
    {
    }
  }
}
```

This is the base class we will start from. At the moment, it does very little aside from store your name from join data, send your Player ID, and broadcast your presence to other players (as well as send you join messages for all existing players).

We'll also create a class to represent our bots using the following code:

```
using System;
using System.Collections.Generic;
using System.Linq;
using System.Text;

namespace BotWarsGame
{
  public class Bot
  {
    public ulong BotID;
    public int OwnerID;

    public float PositionX = 0f;
    public float PositionY = 0f;

    public int Health = 100;

    public Bot( Player owner, ulong botID )
```

```
        {
            this.OwnerID = owner.Id;
            this.BotID = botID;
        }
    }
}
```

You may notice that we aren't generating an ID for our bots. We're going to learn how to generate objects instantly on the client side without server intervention. This will include how to generate a unique object ID on the client. For the time being, we'll continue with the server code and worry about the details of this later.

Let's modify our `Player` class so that the player can own a list of bots.

```
public class Player : BasePlayer
{
  public string Name;

  // the bots this player owns
  public List<Bot> OwnedBots = new List<Bot>();
}
```

And, we'll handle a message that spawns a bot for the player:

```
// This method is called when a player sends a message into the
  server code
Dictionary<ulong,Bot> bots = new Dictionary<ulong,Bot>();
public override void GotMessage( Player player, Message message )
{
  switch( message.Type )
  {
    case "SpawnBot":
    {
      // player spawned a bot
      ulong botID = message.GetULong( 0 );
      float botPosX = message.GetFloat( 1 );
      float botPosY = message.GetFloat( 2 );
      Bot bot = new Bot( player, botID );
      bot.PositionX = botPosX;
      bot.PositionY = botPosY;
      player.OwnedBots.Add( bot );

      // add bot to dictionary so we can later look up bots by ID
      bots.Add( botID, bot );

      // broadcast spawn message to other players
```

```
        foreach( Player pl in Players )
        {
          if( pl == player )
            continue;

          pl.Send( "OnBotSpawned", pl.Id, botID, botPosX, botPosY );
        }
      }
        break;
    }
  }
```

So, on the client side, a player will spawn a bot and send the SpawnBot message to the server. The server will handle this message by adding a new bot to the list of bots the player owns and notifying everyone else that the bot was spawned.

We'll also need to notify new players of all the bots currently spawned, which we'll do in UserJoined:

```
// This method is called whenever a player joins the game
public override void UserJoined( Player player )
{
  player.Name = player.JoinData[ "Name" ];

  // send the player their own ID
  player.Send( "SetID", player.Id );

  // inform everyone that this user has joined
  Broadcast( "UserJoined", player.Id, player.Name );

  // inform the user of everyone else in the room,
  // plus their bots
  foreach( Player p in Players )
  {
    if( p == player )
      continue;

    player.Send( "UserJoined", player.Id, player.Name );

    // notify new player of existing bots
    foreach( Bot bot in p.OwnedBots )
    {
      player.Send( "OnBotSpawned", p.Id, bot.BotID, bot.PositionX,
        bot.PositionY );
    }
  }
}
```

Players will be in control of their own bots (client-authoritative), so we'll accept update messages from players to move bots:

```
// This method is called when a player sends a message into the server
code
public override void GotMessage( Player player, Message message )
{
  switch( message.Type )
  {
    case "SpawnBot":
    {
      // player spawned a bot
      ulong botID = message.GetULong( 0 );
      float botPosX = message.GetFloat( 1 );
      float botPosY = message.GetFloat( 2 );
      Bot bot = new Bot( player, botID );
      bot.PositionX = botPosX;
      bot.PositionY = botPosY;
      player.OwnedBots.Add( bot );

      // broadcast spawn message to other players
      foreach( Player pl in Players )
      {
        if( pl == player )
          continue;
        pl.Send( "OnBotSpawned", pl.Id, botID, botPosX, botPosY );
      }
    }
      break;
    case "UpdateBot":
    {
      // update one of the player's bots
      ulong botID = message.GetULong( 0 );
      float botPosX = message.GetFloat( 1 );
      float botPosY = message.GetFloat( 2 );

      if( bots.ContainsKey( botID ) )
      {
        Bot bot = bots[ botID ];
        bot.PositionX = botPosX;
        bot.PositionY = botPosY;
      }
    }
      break;
  }
}
```

We'll also handle Damage messages for when one unit attacks another.

```csharp
// This method is called when a player sends a message into the
   server code
public override void GotMessage( Player player, Message message )
{
  switch( message.Type )
  {
    case "SpawnBot":
    {
      // player spawned a bot
      ulong botID = message.GetULong( 0 );
      float botPosX = message.GetFloat( 1 );
      float botPosY = message.GetFloat( 2 );
      Bot bot = new Bot( player, botID );
      bot.PositionX = botPosX;
      bot.PositionY = botPosY;
      player.OwnedBots.Add( bot );
      bots.Add( bot.BotID, bot );

      // broadcast spawn message to other players
      foreach( Player pl in Players )
      {
        if( pl == player )
          continue;

        pl.Send( "OnBotSpawned", pl.Id, botID, botPosX, botPosY );
      }
    }
      break;
    case "UpdateBot":
    {
      // update one of the player's bots
      ulong botID = message.GetULong( 0 );
      float botPosX = message.GetFloat( 1 );
      float botPosY = message.GetFloat( 2 );

      if( bots.ContainsKey( botID ) )
      {
        Bot bot = bots[ botID ];
        bot.PositionX = botPosX;
        bot.PositionY = botPosY;
      }
    }
```

```
      break;
  case "TakeDamage":
  {
    // one bot damaged another
    ulong destBotID = message.GetULong( 0 );

    if( bots.ContainsKey( destBotID ) )
    {
      Bot destBot = bots[ destBotID ];
      destBot.Health -= 10;

      // check if the bot died
      if( destBot.Health <= 0 )
      {
        // remove bot from world
        foreach( Player pl in Players )
        {
          if( pl.Id == destBot.OwnerID
          {                        pl.OwnedBots.Remove( destBot );
            break;
          }
        }
        bots.Remove( destBot.BotID );

        // broadcast death message
        Broadcast( "BotDied", destBot.BotID );

        // send got kill message to player sending the damage
          message
        player.Send( "GotKill" );
      }
      else
{
// send new health amount to victim
foreach( Player pl in Players )
{
  if( pl.Id == destBot.OwnerID )
  {
    pl.Send( "TookDamage", destBot.BotID, destBot.Health );
    break;
  }
}
}
}
      }
```

```
        }
          break;
      }
    }
```

We'll also periodically broadcast the state of all bots currently alive. Player.IO has a fairly small bandwidth limit, so we'll do this five times per second (in a twitch-based game you would generally broadcast anywhere from ten to twenty times per second)

We'll hook up a timer in GameStarted to accomplish this:

```
// This method is called when an instance of your the game is
  created
public override void GameStarted()
{
  // broadcast game state 5 times per second
  AddTimer(
    delegate()
    {
      foreach( Player player in Players )
      {
        foreach( Bot bot in player.OwnedBots )
        {

// broadcast bot state (position & health)
        foreach( Player target in Players )
        {
          if( target != player )
          Broadcast( "UpdateBot", bot.BotID, bot.PositionX,
            bot.PositionY, bot.Health );
        }             }
      }
    }, 200 );
}
```

And finally, when a player's bots have all been killed, we will kick them out of the game. We'll modify our TakeDamage message case:

```
case "TakeDamage":
{
  // one bot damaged another
  ulong destBotID = message.GetULong( 0 );
  if( bots.ContainsKey( destBotID ) )
  {
    Bot destBot = bots[ destBotID ];
```

```
        destBot.Health -= 10;
      // check if the bot died
      if( destBot.Health <= 0 )
      {
        // remove bot from world
        foreach( Player pl in Players )
        {
          if( pl.Id == destBot.OwnerID )
          {
            pl.OwnedBots.Remove( destBot );
            // player is out of bots?
            if( pl.OwnedBots.Count == 0 )
            {
              // boot them from the game
              pl.Disconnect();
            }
            break;
          }
        }
        bots.Remove( destBot.BotID );
        // broadcast death message
        Broadcast( "BotDied", destBot.BotID );
        // send got kill message to player sending the damage
          message
        player.Send( "GotKill" );
      }
      else
      {
        // send new health amount to victim
        foreach( Player pl in Players )
        {
          if( pl.Id == destBot.OwnerID )
          {
            pl.Send( "TookDamage", destBot.BotID, destBot.Health );
            break;
          }
        }
      }
    }
  }
  break;
```

We are now finished with our server-side code. Now to work on the client side.

Client-side code

In our game we'll have two scenes. The first scene lets the player choose a name, displays their stats, and lets them join a random room, and the second scene is used for gameplay.

First, we'll need some place to store our client and connection, among other things. Let's create a class with static variables for these.

```
using UnityEngine;
using System.Collections.Generic;

using PlayerIOClient;

public class NetworkUtils : MonoBehaviour
{
  public static Client client;
  public static Connection connection;
  public static DatabaseObject playerObject;
  public static int localPlayerID;
  public static Dictionary<int, string> PlayersInRoom = new
Dictionary<int, string>();
}
```

Now, our `Connect` script can set these values, and we can later retrieve them easily.

The next thing we'll add is a `Connect` script that connects to Player.IO, saves the client, loads the player object, saves that, and displays the player's stats (bots killed, and bots lost), and will additionally join a random room and load the gameplay scene.

```
using UnityEngine;
using System.Collections;
using System.Collections.Generic;

using PlayerIOClient;

public class ConnectScreen : MonoBehaviour
{
  string playerName = "Player";

  bool connecting = true;

  int botsKilled = 0;
  int botsLost = 0;
```

```
void Connect()
{
  // we need some monobehavior in the scene for player.io to
    work, but it can be any monobehavior so we'll just put our
    NetworkUtils component on it.
  if( GameObject.Find( "_playerIO" ) == null )
  {
    GameObject go = new GameObject( "_playerIO" );
    go.AddComponent<NetworkUtils>();
    DontDestroyOnLoad( go );
    PlayerIO.UnityInit( go.GetComponent<NetworkUtils>() );
  }

  PlayerIO.Connect( "YourGameIDHere", "public", playerName,
    null, null,
    delegate( Client client )
    {
      Debug.Log( "Connected" );

      // store client for later retrieval
      NetworkUtils.client = client;

      // load player object
      client.BigDB.LoadMyPlayerObject(
        delegate( DatabaseObject playerObj )
        {
          // store player object for later retrieval
          NetworkUtils.playerObject = playerObj;

          // read stats from player object
          botsKilled = playerObj.GetInt( "Kills", 0 );
          botsLost = playerObj.GetInt( "Deaths", 0 );
        },
        delegate( PlayerIOError error )
        {
          Debug.Log( "Failed loading player object: " +
            error.Message );
        } );
    },
    delegate( PlayerIOError error )
    {
      Debug.Log( "Failed to connect: " + error.Message );
    } );
}
```

```csharp
void JoinRoom()
{
  NetworkUtils.client.Multiplayer.CreateJoinRoom( "$service-
    room$", "GameRoom", true,
    null,
    new Dictionary<string, string> { },
    delegate( Connection connection )
    {
      Debug.Log( "Connected to room" );
      NetworkUtils.connection = connection;

      // load gameplay scene
      Application.LoadLevel( "GameplayScene" );
    },
    delegate( PlayerIOError error )
    {
      Debug.Log( "Failed to join room: " + error.Message );
    } );
}

void OnGUI()
{
  if( !connecting )
  {
    if( NetworkUtils.playerObject != null )
    {
      GUILayout.Label( "Enemy Bots Destroyed: " + botsKilled );
      GUILayout.Label( "Bots Lost: " + botsLost );
      if( GUILayout.Button( "Play", GUILayout.Width( 100f ) ) )
      {
        // join random room
        JoinRoom();
      }
    }
    else
    {
      playerName = GUILayout.TextField( playerName,
        GUILayout.Width( 200f ) );
      if( GUILayout.Button( "Connect", GUILayout.Width( 100f ) )
        )
      {
        Connect();
      }
    }
```

```
    }
    else
    {
      GUILayout.Label( "Connecting..." );
    }
  }
}
```

This code displays a screen allowing the player to enter their name and connect to Player.IO. Once connected, the player's stats are displayed, and the player can click on "Play" to join a service room. After it connects to a room, it loads the "GameplayScene". We'll need to create this scene, and add our gameplay scripts to it.

First, we'll create a script to handle incoming messages:

```
using UnityEngine;
using System.Collections;

public class MessageHandler : MonoBehaviour
{
  void OnEnable()
  {
    NetworkUtils.connection.OnMessage += connection_OnMessage;
    NetworkUtils.connection.OnDisconnect +=
      connection_OnDisconnect;
  }

  // We'll also disconnect our event handlers. This is not
    necessary in some cases, but it is always good practice.
  void OnDisable()
  {
    NetworkUtils.connection.OnMessage -= connection_OnMessage;
    NetworkUtils.connection.OnDisconnect -=
      connection_OnDisconnect;
  }

  void connection_OnDisconnect( object sender, string message )
  {
    Debug.Log( "Disconnected from server" );
    NetworkUtils.connection = null;

    // save player object
    NetworkUtils.playerObject.Save();
```

```
        // go back to main menu
        Application.LoadLevel( "MainMenu" );
    }

    void connection_OnMessage( object sender, PlayerIOClient.
      Message e )
    {
        // handle incoming messages
    }
}
```

All messages sent to us by the server will trigger our `connection_OnMessage` function. Additionally, if the client is disconnected from the server the game will dispose of the `Connection` object, save the player object, and load the main scene.

Next, let's create a component to keep track of the owner ID and instance ID of a bot, so that we always have a way to tell who owns a bot:

```
using UnityEngine;
using System.Collections;
using System.Collections.Generic;

public class BotInfo : MonoBehaviour
{
    // a map of botID -> bot
    public static Dictionary<ulong,BotInfo> botMap =
      new Dictionary<ulong,BotInfo>();

    // the player that owns this bot
    public int OwnerID;

    // the ID of this bot
    public ulong BotID;

    // whether this bot belongs to the local player
    public bool IsMine
    {
        get
        {
            return OwnerID == NetworkUtils.localPlayerID;
        }
    }

    public void Register()
    {
```

```
    botMap.Add( this.BotID, this );
  }

  void OnDestroy()
  {
    botMap.Remove( this.BotID );
  }

  float timer = 0f;
  void Update()
  {
    if( IsMine )
    {
      timer += Time.deltaTime;
      if( timer >= 0.1f )
      {
        // send update message to server
        NetworkUtils.connection.Send( "UpdateBot", BotID,
          transform.position.x, transform.position.z );
      }
    }
  }
}
```

When a bot is spawned we'll set its OwnerID and BotID, and then call Register. Register adds the bot to a dictionary, so later we can look up bots by ID. When the bot is destroyed, it is removed from the dictionary.

Next, we'll handle a few message types:

```
void connection_OnMessage( object sender, PlayerIOClient.
  Message e )
{
  // handle incoming messages
  switch( e.Type )
  {
    // server sent us our ID
    case "SetID":
      NetworkUtils.localPlayerID = e.GetInt( 0 );
      break;
    // add a player to list of players in the room
    case "UserJoined":
      NetworkUtils.PlayersInRoom.Add( e.GetInt( 0 ), e.GetString
        ( 1 ) );
      break;
```

```
        // remove player from list of players
        case "UserLeft":
          NetworkUtils.PlayersInRoom.Remove( e.GetInt( 0 ) );
          //clean up this player's bots
          foreach( ulong botID in BotInfo.botMap.Keys )
          {
            Destroy( BotInfo.botMap[ botID ].gameObject );
          }
          break;
        // spawn a bot
        case "OnBotSpawned":
          break;
        // update a bot
        case "UpdateBot":
          break;
        // destroy a bot
        case "BotDied":
          break;
        // local player got a kill
        case "GotKill":
          break;
        // one of local player's bots took damage
        case "TookDamage":
          break;
    }
}
```

Currently, this handles the server sending us our ID (this is stored in `NetworkUtils`, which is important in order to know which bots belong to us), users joining (the user's name is stored in a dictionary so we can look up the player name by ID), and leaving. We also have stubs for gameplay-related messages, which we'll start filling in.

```
public GameObject BotPrefab;
void connection_OnMessage( object sender, PlayerIOClient.
  Message e )
{
  // handle incoming messages
  switch( e.Type )
  {
    // server sent us our ID
    case "SetID":
      NetworkUtils.localPlayerID = e.GetInt( 0 );
      break;
    // add a player to list of players in the room
```

```
  case "UserJoined":
    NetworkUtils.PlayersInRoom.Add( e.GetInt( 0 ), e.GetString( 1 )
);
    break;
  // remove player from list of players
  case "UserLeft":
    NetworkUtils.PlayersInRoom.Remove( e.GetInt( 0 ) );
    //clean up this player's bots
    foreach( ulong botID in BotInfo.botMap.Keys )
    {
      Destroy( BotInfo.botMap[ botID ].gameObject );
    }
    break;
  // spawn a bot
  case "OnBotSpawned":
    int spawnedBotOwnerID = e.GetInt( 0 );
    ulong spawnedBotID = e.GetULong( 1 );
    float spawnedBotPosX = e.GetFloat( 2 );
    float spawnedBotPosY = e.GetFloat( 3 );

    GameObject bot = (GameObject)Instantiate( BotPrefab, new
      Vector3( spawnedBotPosX, 0f, spawnedBotPosY ),
      Quaternion.identity );
    bot.GetComponent<BotInfo>().OwnerID = spawnedBotOwnerID;
    bot.GetComponent<BotInfo>().BotID = spawnedBotID;
    bot.GetComponent<BotInfo>().Register();
    break;
  // update a bot
  case "UpdateBot":
    ulong updateBotID = e.GetULong( 0 );
    float updatePosX = e.GetFloat( 1 );
    float updatePosY = e.GetFloat( 2 );
    int updateBotHealth = e.GetInt( 3 );

    BotInfo updateBot = BotInfo.botMap[ updateBotID ];
    updateBot.transform.position = new Vector3( updatePosX,
      0f, updatePosY );
    updateBot.SendMessage( "SetHealth", updateBotHealth,
      SendMessageOptions.DontRequireReceiver );
    break;
  // destroy a bot
  case "BotDied":
    // kill bot
    ulong killedBotID = e.GetULong( 0 );
```

```
        BotInfo killedBot = BotInfo.botMap[ killedBotID ];
        if( killedBot.IsMine )
        {
          // increment lost bots
          NetworkUtils.playerObject.Set( "Deaths",
            NetworkUtils.playerObject.GetInt( "Deaths" ) + 1 );
        }

        // destroy bot obj
        GameObject.Destroy( killedBot );
        break;
      // local player got a kill
      case "GotKill":
        // increment kills
        NetworkUtils.playerObject.Set( "Kills",
          NetworkUtils.playerObject.GetInt( "Kills" ) + 1 );
        break;
      // one of local player's bots took damage
      case "TookDamage":
        Debug.Log( "Taking damage!" );
        break;
    }
  }
```

This is mostly straightforward, the Spawn Bot message instantiates a bot prefab and assigns network IDs, the update and death messages look up the appropriate bot by ID and call methods/set properties, GotKill increments the number of kills, and so on. Most of the code should be self-explanatory at this point.

Next, we'll create the script for bots. This script will allow us to select a single bot with left-click, and order that bot with right click. If we click the ground, the bot will move to that spot. Otherwise, if we click on another bot that isn't ours, the bot will move to within range and attack (send damage messages).

```
using UnityEngine;
using System.Collections;

public class BotScript : MonoBehaviour
{
  public static BotScript SelectedBot;

  private Vector3 targetMovePos;
  private BotInfo targetEnemy;

  private float attackTimer = 0f;
```

```
void Awake()
{
  targetMovePos = Vector3.zero;
}

void Update()
{
  // left mouse button pressed?
  if( Input.GetMouseButtonDown( 0 ) )
  {
    // raycast
    RaycastHit hit;
    if( Physics.Raycast( Camera.main.ScreenPointToRay( Input.
      mousePosition ), out hit ) )
    {
      BotInfo hitBot = hit.collider.GetComponent<BotInfo>();
      if( hitBot != null && hitBot.IsMine )
      {
        // select bot
        SelectedBot = hitBot.GetComponent<BotScript>();
      }
    }
  }

  if( !GetComponent<BotInfo>().IsMine )
    return;

// current target not null? move towards and attack
  if( targetEnemy != null )
  {
    moveTowards( targetEnemy.transform.position, 2f );
    targetMovePos = transform.position;

    // close enough to target? attack
    if( Vector3.Distance( transform.position,
      targetEnemy.transform.position ) <= 2f )
    {
      attackTimer += Time.deltaTime;
      if( attackTimer >= 1f )
      {
        attackTimer = 0f;
        // send damage message
        NetworkUtils.connection.Send( "TakeDamage",
          targetEnemy.BotID );
```

```
        }
      }
    }
    else
    {
      moveTowards( targetMovePos, 0.5f );
    }

    if( SelectedBot != this )
      return;

    // right mouse button pressed?
    if( Input.GetMouseButtonDown( 1 ) )
    {
      // raycast
      RaycastHit hit;
      if( Physics.Raycast( Camera.main.ScreenPointToRay( Input.
        mousePosition ), out hit ) )
      {
        BotInfo hitBot = hit.collider.GetComponent<BotInfo>();
        if( hitBot != null && !hitBot.IsMine )
        {
          // target selected bot
          targetEnemy = hitBot;
        }
        else if( hitBot == null )
        {
          // move to position
          targetMovePos = hit.point;
        }
      }
    }
  }

  // move to within a certain distance of the target
  void moveTowards( Vector3 pos, float range )
  {
    if( Vector3.Distance( transform.position, pos ) > range )
    {
      // move toward at 5 meters per second
      transform.position = Vector3.MoveTowards( transform.position,
        pos, Time.deltaTime * 5f );
    }
  }
}
```

We'll attach this to a cube alongside the `BotInfo` component and save it as a prefab.

Next, we'll spawn our bots in the scene at five predetermined spawn points. For the purposes of learning, our game is client-authoritative, and this includes generating object IDs. What we're doing here is basing the ID off of the player's ID (four bytes are player ID, the other four bytes are just an incrementing counter), which is why we used an unsigned long for the bot ID. As the player ID is unique for each player, we have a fairly painless way to generate instant network-unique client-side IDs.

```
using UnityEngine;
using System.Collections;

public class SpawnBots : MonoBehaviour
{
  public GameObject BotPrefab;

  public Transform[] SpawnPoints;

  private int lastGeneratedBotID = 0;

  IEnumerator Start()
  {
    // 3 second prepare time
    yield return new WaitForSeconds( 3f );

    foreach( Transform spawn in SpawnPoints )
    {
      ulong botID = AllocateBotID();

      GameObject bot = (GameObject)Instantiate( BotPrefab, new
        Vector3( spawn.position.x, 0f, spawn.position.z ),
        Quaternion.identity );
      bot.GetComponent<BotInfo>().OwnerID =
        NetworkUtils.localPlayerID;
      bot.GetComponent<BotInfo>().BotID = botID;

      // send spawn message to server
      NetworkUtils.connection.Send( "SpawnBot", botID,
        spawn.position.x, spawn.position.z );
    }
  }

  ulong AllocateBotID()
  {
```

```
        // here, we will generate a unique network ID for one of our
          bots
        // to do this without server intervention, the ID will be
          based on the Player ID (which is guaranteed to be unique per
          player)
        // four of the bytes will be player ID, and the other four
          bytes will be bot instance ID
        ulong id = (ulong)lastGeneratedBotID++;          // int fills
          four bytes, leaving a remaining four
        id |= ( (ulong)NetworkUtils.localPlayerID << 4 );  // shift
          player ID to fill the remaining four bytes

        return id;
    }
}
```

At this point, we are nearly done. We just have to set up our gameplay scene. This is a fairly simple matter, just drop in a plane (make sure *Y* is set to *0*) for the floor, and create starting points for each of the bots as empty game objects (these are then dropped onto the spawn array for the SpawnBot script, in addition to our bot prefab).

And now, our Bot Wars example game is complete.

Summary

In this chapter, we learned about another server technology known as Player.IO. Player.IO differs from Photon in that it's better suited to room-based setups and smaller Flash-type games, rather than network-heavy twitch games or massively multiplayer games. It also cannot be self-hosted, similar to Photon Cloud.

We have learned how to connect, join rooms, send and receive messages, and work with BigDB for persisting player data. We then applied this knowledge in creating a pseudo-RTS demo where the player can command 5 units to attack other player-controlled units. In the process, we also learned how we can generate a unique 64 bit ID on the client with no server intervention by using a 32 bit player ID.

In the next chapter, we'll cover our final networking system, an HTTP push service known as PubNub.

5
PubNub – The Global Chatbox

In this chapter, we will be covering a radically different networking system known as **PubNub**. PubNub differs from most traditional networking systems, in which it uses HTTP to communicate, rather than straight TCP or UDP sockets. While PubNub does not work well for twitch-based games requiring low latency or authoritative server setups, it is just fine for other forms of communication such as instant messaging.

In this chapter, we'll learn:

- How PubNub works over HTTP
- Parsing JSON returned from PubNub
- Building a WWW wrapper around PubNub
- Creating a global chatbox application

Overview of PubNub

Unlike traditional TCP or UDP communication methods, PubNub is based around HTTP. Users are divided by application, into channels. Within each channel, users can publish messages, which are broadcast to all users in the channel. There are some limitations in this regard. It is not possible to direct a message to a specific user within a channel, and this message is stored in a plain text format. **Latency** is also a major factor, as messages can take some time to be received. These factors make PubNub unsuitable for games requiring fast and efficient communication, but it has other uses. For instance, if players cannot be directly connected to each other to communicate (for instance, for an instant messaging feature), it's possible to use specially named channels based on the user ID to send messages to players (each player listens on their own dedicated channel for incoming private messages).

Getting started

Before we continue, you'll need to sign up for an account at PubNub. Navigate to the following URL to sign up for a free account:

```
http://www.pubnub.com/free-trial
```

After you've logged in, you'll need to create a new app as shown in the following screenshot:

Under the **More Apps** menu, select **create new app**. Enter a name and hit *Enter*.

After the app is created, there should be a section containing two important pieces of information:

- Your Publish Key
- Your Subscribe Key

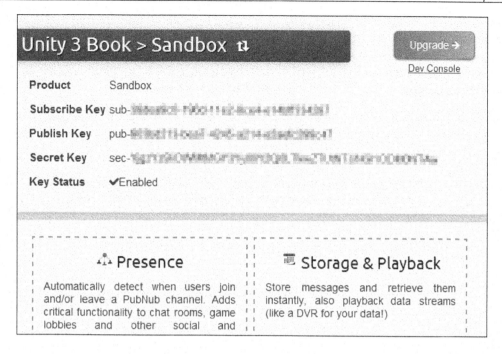

- The Publish and Subscribe keys are both needed in order to publish messages to PubNub and receive messages from PubNub.

Now that you have these two things, we can get started.

How PubNub works

As mentioned earlier, PubNub works over HTTP rather than TCP or UDP sockets. This means, the PubNub service is entirely interacted with via a web service. How does this work?

There are two URLs which form all interactions with PubNub. One is used for publishing. You request this URL and pass all information such as Publish key, Subscribe key, the channel to publish on, and the message to publish, and so on.

The other URL is used for subscribing. For the best latency, you make a request to this URL, and as soon as it returns something you make another request, and so on. Unlike most web requests, this URL has an especially long time out, and won't return anything until somebody else publishes a message on that channel. That means you generally only make requests after you receive a message.

When you request the subscribe URL, you pass a few bits of information just as with publishing, with the addition of a "time token". The first time you request it, you pass a time token of 0. This tells PubNub to give you the current time token. Every time you get a response from the subscribed URL, you store the time token and use that for the next request. This ensures that you don't get old messages.

PubNub's subscribed URL will return JSON, so before we write our wrapper around PubNub we'll need a way to parse JSON.

JSON (JavaScript Object Notation) is a format for storing structured data stored as key/value pairs. For instance, a simple JSON object might look like this:

```
{"key1":value1, "key2":value2, ... "key n":value n}
```

Values can be of several types such as Booleans, integers, floats, and so on. They can also be arrays, or nested objects.

For more information, check out the following resource on the JSON format:

```
http://www.json.org/
```

This method of communication, using a request/response system, can have a big impact on any networking built on top of it. Keep in mind, this request/response system of HTTP is designed for browsers to request web pages from a server, not necessarily for real-time communication. In addition, while HTTP is implemented with TCP, it is not the same thing as TCP. It carries lots of information designed to fetch resources from a web server, rather than sending/receiving general purpose messages. In particular, the browser URL or the POST parameters are the only methods available to the client to pass any data to the server. Additionally, a whole host of other information will be sent as part of the request, such as user agent (what browser is requesting the data), the content type the client expects, language, content length, and more. This could potentially lead to fairly large messages being passed around. In general, while PubNub can be invaluable for some things that don't need to be instant such as lobby room chat, it does not make a good candidate for real-time multiplayers. Additionally, one benefit of using HTTP is that firewalls are generally configured to allow most web traffic through—there is significantly less danger of the firewall blocking game network traffic (such as on corporate networks).

Parsing JSON from PubNub

All responses from the subscribe service are structured as follows:

- An array, containing:
  - ° An array of new messages since the last call to subscribe
  - ° A new time token to use for the next call

The first time you make a request to subscribe, you get something like this:

```
[[],"13782280489181338"]
```

This is a JSON array. The first is an array of messages—for the first request, it will be empty. The second entry is a string, and it is the new time token to use.

After the first request, you'll see something that looks more like this:

```
[[ "Some message here", "Another message here" ], "13782280489181345"]
```

Now, the first entry isn't full. It's an array of strings (in fact, these are JSON data which means they can hold any data you want, but in the case of our chat application we are sending string values). These are all of the new messages which have been published to the channel since the last time you subscribed.

To parse this, we'll use a JSON parser made for Unity called SimpleJSON. It can be downloaded for free from the Unify Community wiki, here:

http://wiki.unity3d.com/index.php/SimpleJSON

Follow the setup instructions to add it to a Unity project.

Next, let's build a helper function for parsing PubNub responses:

```csharp
using UnityEngine;
using System.Collections;

using SimpleJSON;

public class PubNubUtils
{
  public static string[] ParseSubscribeResponse( string response,
    out string timeToken )
  {
    // parse the JSON as a JSON array
    var json = JSON.Parse( response ).AsArray;
```

```
      // first entry is another JSON array
      var messages = json[ 0 ].AsArray;

      // second entry is new time token
      timeToken = json[ 1 ].Value;

      // parse message JSON array into string array
      string[] ret = new string[ messages.Count ];
      for( int i = 0; i < ret.Length; i++ )
      {
        ret[ i ] = messages[ i ].Value;
      }
      // return messages
      return ret;
    }
  }
```

Now that we can take the response from subscribe and parse a list of messages and the new time token, let's build our wrapper around PubNub.

Building a PubNub interface

Our system will make use of the built-in WWW class of Unity to make requests, and a very useful Unity script feature known as **coroutines** to asynchronously wait until the request is finished — since a web request can take a while to complete, we do not want our game loop to be paused while waiting for the server to respond.

> In Unity, a coroutine is a way to semi-asynchronously execute some code by dividing the function into steps which can be performed across multiple frames. Coroutines "yield" values during execution. This value is interpreted by Unity and used to determine when to resume the coroutine. For instance, yielding null will cause Unity to pause our function and resume it on the next frame. In this case, we can yield a WWW object, which will cause Unity to pause our function and resume it once the WWW request has finished (the WWW request itself is handled asynchronously in the background).

First, we'll create a `MonoBehaviour` class to accomplish this. It will store the necessary keys, and make the needed requests, as well as keep a static reference to the current instance:

```
using UnityEngine;
using System.Collections;
using System.Collections.Generic;
```

```
public class PubNubWrapper : MonoBehaviour
{
  public static PubNubWrapper instance;

  public string PublishKey = "";
  public string SubscribeKey = "";

  private Dictionary<string, System.Action<string>>
    channelMessageHandlers = new Dictionary<string,
    System.Action<string>>();

  private string timeToken = "0";

  void Awake()
  {
    instance = this;
  }

  // publish a message to the given channel
  public void Publish( string message, string channel )
  {
  }

  // subscribe to receive messages from the given channel
  public void Subscribe( string channel, System.Action<string>
    messageHandler )
  {
  }

  // unsubscribe to stop receiving messages from the given channel
  public void Unsubscribe( string channel )
  {
  }
}
```

Right now it does nothing, but we'll begin filling in the functions. First, we'll create the publish function:

```
// publish a message to the given channel
public void Publish( string message, string channel )
{
  // escape the message so we can put it in a URL
  string escapedMessage = WWW.EscapeURL( message ).Replace( "+",
    "%20" ); // Unity's URL escaping function replaces space with
    '+'. It's better on some platforms to use %20
```

```
// form the URL
// http://pubsub.pubnub.com
// /publish
// /[publish key]
// /[subscribe key]
// /0
// /[channel name]
// /0
// /[JSON message data]
string url =
  "http://pubsub.pubnub.com" +
  "/publish" +
  "/" + PublishKey +
  "/" + SubscribeKey +
  "/0" +
  "/" + channel +
  "/0" +
  "/\"" + escapedMessage + "\"";

// make the request
WWW www = new WWW( url );
}
```

This is fairly straightforward. The data for the publish call is formatted as a URL, containing among other things the Publish key, the channel to publish on, and the message to publish. Note that the message is wrapped in quotes—remember that the message we post is actually a JSON object, not simply a string. In this case, we are simply formatting it as a JSON string. We create a new WWW object with the URL to actually make the request, which publishes the message.

Next, the subscribe function. This one will actually kick off a coroutine, this coroutine will run in a loop making subscribe requests to PubNub. If when one of these requests is finished, the callback is not present in the dictionary, that must mean Unsubscribe was called, so we simply break out of the coroutine.

```
// subscribe to receive messages from the given channel
public void Subscribe( string channel, System.Action<string>
messageHandler )
{
  channelMessageHandlers.Add( channel, messageHandler );
  StartCoroutine( doSubscribe( channel ) );
}

IEnumerator doSubscribe( string channel )
{
```

```
    // as long as we have a message handler for the given channel (we're
subscribed), keep making requests
    while( channelMessageHandlers.ContainsKey( channel ) )
    {
      // form the URL
      // http://pubsub.pubnub.com
      // /subscribe
      // /[subscribe key here]
      // /[channel name here]
      // /0
      // /[time token here]
      string url =
        "http://pubsub.pubnub.com" +
        "/subscribe" +
        "/" + SubscribeKey +
        "/" + channel +
        "/0" +
        "/" + timeToken;

      // make the request
      WWW www = new WWW( url );

      // in Unity, we can yield a WWW object,
      // which makes Unity "pause" this coroutine
      // until the request has either encountered an error
      // or finished.
      yield return www;

      // www.error is a string
      // it will either be null/empty if there is no error, or it
      // will contain the error message if there was one.
      if( !string.IsNullOrEmpty( www.error ) )
      {
        // log the error to the console
        Debug.LogWarning( "Subscribe failed: " + www.error );

        // unsubscribe from the channel,
        // we don't want error messages spamming the console.
        Unsubscribe( channel );

        // yield break causes Unity to stop exiting this
        // coroutine. It is equivalent to "return;" in
        // a regular method.
        yield break;
```

```
    }

    // parse the response
    string newToken;
    // parse the response from the server
    // returned is an array of new messages posted since we
    // last made a request
    string[] newMessages = PubNubUtils.ParseSubscribeResponse(
      www.text, out newToken );

    // store the returned time token
    // this is important to ensure we only get new messages
    timeToken = newToken;

    // make sure we're still subscribed to this channel
    if( channelMessageHandlers.ContainsKey( channel ) )
    {
      // handle each message separately
      for( int i = 0; i < newMessages.Length; i++ )
      {
        channelMessageHandlers[ channel ]( newMessages[ i ] );
      }
    }
  }
}
```

And finally, the unsubscribe method. This will simply remove the callback associated with a given channel, which will break out of the doSubscribe coroutine loop.

```
// unsubscribe to stop receiving messages from the given channel
public void Unsubscribe( string channel )
{
  channelMessageHandlers.Remove( channel );
}
```

We now have a functional wrapper around PubNub. To test this, we'll do a simple script that posts a message to a channel, and listens on the same channel logging received messages to the console.

```
using UnityEngine;
using System.Collections;

public class PubNubTest : MonoBehaviour
{
  void Start()
```

```
    {
        PubNubWrapper.instance.Subscribe( "HelloWorld",
            delegate( string message )
            {
                Debug.Log( "Received message: " + message );
            } );

        PubNubWrapper.instance.Publish( "Hello, world!", "HelloWorld" );
    }
}
```

If you place this script, as well as PubNubWrapper, in a scene and click on **Play**
you'll see after a short delay **Received message: Hello, world!** printed to the console.
Note that you'll need to paste your Publish and Subscribe keys into the fields in the
PubNubWrapper inspector, like this:

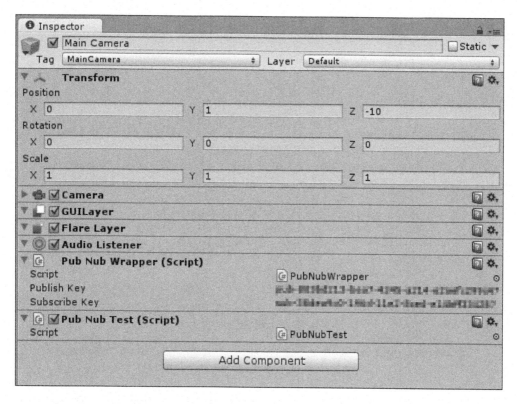

Now that we have a framework built around PubNub, let's get started creating
a global chatbox application.

Creating a global chatbox application

In many ways, our global chatbox will look a lot like the chatbox that we built in Photon. However, rather than having separate chatrooms, we'll create one single global chatbox for everyone. There will also be major API differences to keep in mind — in Photon, we were able to use RPCs to conveniently call a function on all connected clients which handled chat messages. However, in PubNub we will need to handle incoming messages, parse them, and process them as chat messages.

In this chatbox example, we'll expand our chatbox with extra functions such as the /me command. Additionally, you'll be able to change your name (which will be announced to the room):

```
using UnityEngine;
using System.Collections;

public class Chatbox : MonoBehaviour
{
  private string PlayerName;
  private string _playerName;

  void Start()
  {
    // we'll assign a random guest name to the player, or load up
      their last name from player prefs
    PlayerName = PlayerPrefs.GetString( "PlayerName", "Guest" +
    Random.Range( 0, 9999 ) );

    // we use a temporary _playerName to pass to
      GUILayout.TextField so that we avoid changing our actual
      name until we've hit the "Change" button.
    _playerName = PlayerName;

    // subscribe to the chatroom.
    // if you wanted, you could easily create separate chatrooms,
      allow the user to pick a chatroom and simply insert the name
      of the chatroom here.
    PubNubWrapper.instance.Subscribe( "Chatbox", HandleMessage );
  }

  // for now we'll simply log messages to the console for testing.
  void HandleMessage( string message )
  {
    Debug.Log( message );
  }
```

```
void OnGUI()
{
  _playerName = GUILayout.TextField( _playerName,
    GUILayout.Width( 200f ) );
  if( GUILayout.Button( "Change Name", GUILayout.Width( 200f
    ) ) )
  {
    // inform everyone else in the room that the player has
      changed their name.
    PubNubWrapper.instance.Publish( PlayerName + " changed
      their name to " + _playerName, "Chatbox" );

    // assign the new name
    PlayerName = _playerName;
  }
}

void OnApplicationQuit()
{
  // when the player quits, save their name to player prefs
    so when they come back later it's saved for them.
  PlayerPrefs.SetString( "PlayerName", PlayerName );
}
}
```

Let's step through this script. Firstly, we load a player name, or generate a new one. We then subscribe to the Chatbox channel. In OnGUI, we draw a text field for the player's name and a "Change Name" button. When the player changes their name, it's announced to the chatroom and the player's name is set. Upon quitting, the name is saved. Received messages are debug logged to the console.

Publishing chat messages

Next, let's add a text field for publishing messages to the chatbox.

First, we'll add a variable to store the value of the text field. On clicking the **Send** button, the text entered by the user is broadcast to the channel and cleared:

```
private string chatText = "";
```

We'll add the text field to the end of our OnGUI call as follows:

```
GUILayout.BeginHorizontal( GUILayout.Width( Screen.width ) );
{
  chatText = GUILayout.TextField( chatText, GUILayout.ExpandWidth(
true ) );
```

```
    if( GUILayout.Button( "Send", GUILayout.Width( 100f ) ) )
    {
        // publish the message the player typed as:
        // [playername]: [message]
        PubNubWrapper.instance.Publish( PlayerName + ": " + chatText,
  "Chatbox" );
        // clear the textbox
        chatText = "";
    }
}
GUILayout.EndHorizontal();
```

Now you can enter text in the text field and hit **Send**, and you'll soon see the message logged to the console.

Right now it always prefixes the message with your name, but let's change this to support the common /me command. In our GUI Send button code, we'll make a simple change:

```
if( GUILayout.Button( "Send", GUILayout.Width( 100f ) ) )
{
    // did the player type a message like this:
    // /me [message]?
    // If so, publish as:
    // [playername] [message] without the colon.
    if( chatText.StartsWith( "/me " ) )
    {
        chatText = chatText.Replace( "/me", "" );
        PubNubWrapper.instance.Publish( PlayerName + chatText,
            "Chatbox" );
    }
    else
    {
            // publish the message the player typed as:
            // [playername]: [message]     PubNubWrapper.instance.
                Publish( PlayerName + ": " + chatText, "Chatbox" );
    }
}
        chatText = "";"";}
```

We simply check if the text begins with "/me", and if so we send the player's name appended to the text without the colon. The full script so far is as follows:

```
using UnityEngine;
using System.Collections;
```

```
public class Chatbox : MonoBehaviour
{
  private string PlayerName;
  private string _playerName;

  private string chatText = "";

  void Start()
  {
    // we'll assign a random guest name to the player, or load up
      their last name from player prefs
    PlayerName = PlayerPrefs.GetString( "PlayerName", "Guest" +
      Random.Range( 0, 9999 ) );

    // we use a temporary _playerName to pass to
      GUILayout.TextField so that we avoid changing our actual
      name until we've hit the "Change" button.
    _playerName = PlayerName;

    // subscribe to the chatroom.
    // if you wanted, you could easily create separate chatrooms,
      allow the user to pick a chatroom and simply insert the
      name of the chatroom here.
    PubNubWrapper.instance.Subscribe( "Chatbox", HandleMessage );
  }

  // for now we'll simply log messages to the console for testing.
  void HandleMessage( string message )
  {
    Debug.Log( message );
  }

  void OnGUI()
  {
    _playerName = GUILayout.TextField( _playerName,
      GUILayout.Width( 200f ) );
    if( GUILayout.Button( "Change Name", GUILayout.Width( 200f ) )
      )
    {
      // inform everyone else in the room that the player has
        changed their name.
      PubNubWrapper.instance.Publish( PlayerName + " changed
        their name to " + _playerName, "Chatbox" );

      // assign the new name
```

```
        PlayerName = _playerName;
    }

    GUILayout.BeginHorizontal( GUILayout.Width( Screen.width ) );
    {
      chatText = GUILayout.TextField( chatText,
        GUILayout.ExpandWidth( true ) );
      if( GUILayout.Button( "Send", GUILayout.Width( 100f ) ) )
      {
        // did the player type a message like this:
        // /me [message]?
        // If so, publish as:
        // [playername] [message] without the colon.
        if( chatText.StartsWith( "/me " ) )
        {
          chatText = chatText.Replace( "/me", "" );
          PubNubWrapper.instance.Publish( PlayerName + chatText,
            "Chatbox" );
        }
        else
        {
        // publish the message the player typed as:
        // [playername]: [message]
          PubNubWrapper.instance.Publish( PlayerName + ": " +
            chatText, "Chatbox" );
        }
        chatText = "";
      }
    }
    GUILayout.EndHorizontal();
  }

  void OnApplicationQuit()
  {
    PlayerPrefs.SetString( "PlayerName", PlayerName );
  }
}
```

Displaying chat logs

We've finished our basic text commands, so next we'll work on displaying the received messages.

We'll add received messages to a "List" of strings, and display these in a scroll view.

First, we'll add some variables:

```
private List<string> messages = new List<string>();
private Vector2 scrollPosition = Vector2.zero;
```

Next, in our HandleMessage function we'll add the message to our list and update the scroll position:

```
void HandleMessage( string message )
{
  Debug.Log( message );
  messages.Add( message );

  // too many messages? Remove the oldest one
  if( messages.Count > 100 )
    messages.RemoveAt( 0 );

  // Unity clamps the scroll value. Setting it sufficiently high will
cause it to scroll to bottom.
  scrolPosition.y = messages.Count * 100f;
}
```

And finally, in our OnGUI method we'll display the message list in a scroll view:

```
void OnGUI()
{
  _playerName = GUILayout.TextField( _playerName,
    GUILayout.Width( 200f ) );
  if( GUILayout.Button( "Change Name", GUILayout.Width( 200f ) ) )
  {
    PubNubWrapper.instance.Publish( PlayerName + " changed their
      name to " + _playerName, "Chatbox" );
    PlayerName = _playerName;
  }

  scrollPosition = GUILayout.BeginScrollView( scrollPosition,
    GUILayout.Width( Screen.width ), GUILayout.Height
    ( Screen.height - 75f ) );
  {
    // display each message
    for( int i = 0; i < messages.Count; i++ )
    {
      GUILayout.Label( messages[ i ] );
    }
  }
  GUILayout.EndScrollView();
```

```
GUILayout.BeginHorizontal( GUILayout.Width( Screen.width ) );
{
  chatText = GUILayout.TextField( chatText,
    GUILayout.ExpandWidth( true ) );
  if( GUILayout.Button( "Send", GUILayout.Width( 100f ) ) )
  {
    if( chatText.StartsWith( "/me " ) )
    {
      chatText = chatText.Replace( "/me", "" );
      PubNubWrapper.instance.Publish( PlayerName +
        chatText, "Chatbox" );
    }
    else
    {
      PubNubWrapper.instance.Publish( PlayerName + ": " +
        chatText, "Chatbox" );
    }
    chatText = "";
  }
}
GUILayout.EndHorizontal();
}
```

At this point, you now have a fully functional global chatbox made with PubNub. You should now know everything you need to send and receive messages. Some modifications you could make are as follows:

- Convert your messages to JSON rather than plain text. This allows you to associate all kinds of extra data with a message, such as who sent a message, what time it was sent, and so on.

- Add a whisper function. Converting messages to JSON will make this easier. The chatbox could include "Whisper/Say" tabs. When in Whisper mode, users enter the name of another user to whisper to. Only that user will receive the message.

- Add profile pictures. Users can set their picture URL, and messages they sent will have their picture next to it (if any). Additionally, you could integrate the "Gravatar.com" service by allowing users to specify their email, and calculating their avatar URL.

Gravatar is a service for avatars which allows users to tie an avatar to their email address for use by multiple services. Avatar images are requested by calculating an MD5 hash from the user's email address, then using the hash to request an image via:

```
http://www.gravatar.com/avatar/HASH
```

For more information on requesting Gravatar images, see:

```
http://en.gravatar.com/site/implement/images/
```

Summary

In this chapter, we learned about a different method of communication based around HTTP web services, and learned about an HTTP communication service known as PubNub. PubNub is good for group communication and passing simple messages around, rather than multiplayer networking. It also has the advantage of communicating over HTTP, which is allowed by most firewalls (such as school or corporate networks).

We learned how to publish messages to channels, and subscribe to receive messages from a channel. We applied this knowledge to creating a global chatbox application where users can talk to each other.

In the next chapters, we'll begin covering more advanced networking concepts, starting with interpolating networked entities, and client-side prediction.

6
Entity Interpolation and Prediction

In nearly all games that employ multiplayer networking, entities need to be interpolated to hide lag and jittery updates. While the updates for an entity only arrive relatively few times per second, and may even be dropped if using UDP, the interpolation needs to smooth these and make the final motion appear smooth, and close to the original player's movements.

Previously, we implemented a simple form of interpolation, by simply interpolating toward the current network position. This looks sluggish and artificial in many cases, especially in twitch-style action games where players move quickly and can change direction on a dime. In this chapter, we'll learn how to implement a form of entity interpolation inspired by the source game engine, employed in a wide variety of AAA games.

In many games, it's also very common to give the server full control over everything. We did this in the chapter on Photon Server, but notice that when the player moved, it took a while before the commands reached the player and movement felt sluggish as a result. In this chapter, we'll learn about a way to solve this using client-side prediction, using methods also inspired by the source game engine, the engine created by Valve to power games such as Left 4 Dead, Portal, and Team Fortress 2, and the upcoming Titanfall.

Entity interpolation

So, we need a way to interpolate entities in a way that is smooth and doesn't appear sluggish to the player (for instance, it should appear to accurately replicate another player's actions faithfully). Let's take a look at how this is done in the source game engine by Valve Studios.

By default source sends twenty snapshots per second. Objects only being viewed at these positions would result in approximately 20 FPS animation, not ideal. In Unity Networking the default send rate is 15, so it would look even worse.

The way source solves this is by introducing a constant view delay of 100 ms. By doing so, under normal circumstances there are always two snapshots available to interpolate between even if a snapshot is lost (due to packet loss). So, as long as the networking engine has a concept of network time, you can use the current network time to interpolate between these two snapshots.

This scheme handles dropped packets fairly well. Under normal circumstances, a dropped packet or two simply means a larger interpolation step (by using network time to interpolate between two packets, we ensure that the interpolation time is always correct). In the rare case that more than one packet in a row is dropped, the entity may pause for a very short duration.

The client-side prediction

If a game employs server-authoritative physics, it usually also needs to employ client-side prediction of player-controlled objects in order to hide the effects of lag. However, this is a more difficult problem than it appears at the outset.

Let's say the server periodically broadcasts the state of all objects. If a player is predicting their own object (and sending inputs to the server), what happens when the player receives a server update? Usually, especially when moving, they snap backward to where they were a moment ago in a motion deemed "rubber-banding". This is because there is always a lag between the client and server.

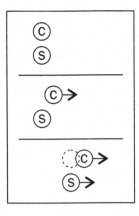

- Client sends input to server and begins moving (resulting in picture 2).

- Server receives message and starts moving player (resulting in picture 3).

- Server sends current position to client (snapping client back to the old position as shown by the dotted circle). The way Source engine and other games handle this involves a fair bit of bookkeeping, but in essence it isn't so hard.

Firstly, the client sends input to the server. The client begins applying this input, and additionally saves the input to a buffer. The message it sends to the server also contains the result of the input, such as position.

When the server receives the input, it applies the input to the player object, and then compares the result with what the client sent as the result. If the client computes the wrong result (for instance, the position sent by the client is too far off the server position), the server sends a message to the client telling the client what is the real result.

When the client receives this correction, it will have been sent some time ago, so the client needs to figure out what the current state is. To do this, it rewinds back to that point, and uses the inputs it stored to replay up to the current state. Essentially, you can think of this as "changing the past" — we're trying to simulate the effects of going back in time and changing the result of a calculation.

One of the most important things to remember about client-side prediction is that, it requires the predicted code to be entirely deterministic — given the same input, it needs to have the same output. Your client and server not only need to run the exact same code with the exact same inputs, you also often need to ensure this code is run in the exact same order (for example, if your client gathers input then updates, while your server updates then gathers input, you'll have plenty of problems).

Rigidbody simulation

If you read through this chapter, you may notice we do not cover rigid bodies.

There's a reason for this. At the moment, Unity's built-in physics do not support manually stepping physics. Manually stepping the simulation is crucial for both client-side prediction, as well as server-side logic. Since we can't accurately step rigid bodies, we can't perform client-side prediction on them.

However, if your game relies on Rigid body simulation (for instance, if players are in control of vehicles), and you require client-side prediction, one possible solution is to integrate a third-party physics engine. This will require some work, but will give you the most control over how the world is stepped, when, and so on. There are a wide variety of free and opensource third-party physics engines written in .NET, such as the Jitter physics engine, or Henge3D. Many of these were designed for use with Microsoft's XNA toolkit, but some are framework-agnostic.

Again, integrating a third-party physics engine is not a task to be taken lightly, but if you need Rigid body simulation with server-authoritative movement it may prove necessary.

Most C# engines are based on (and require) XNA framework classes and will not work in Unity. However, the Jitter engine is one of the few that is completely self-contained. You can check out Jitter at: `http://jitter-physics.com/wordpress/`.

Creating a networked object

Before we can apply interpolation or prediction, we'll need a base to build off of. We'll create a networked object which can be moved around via arrow keys. We'll start with absolutely no interpolation whatsoever—the object instantly appears at the newest location received over the network.

First, let's create a very simple player script.

```
using UnityEngine;
using System.Collections;

public class Player : MonoBehaviour
{
  public float MoveSpeed = 5f;

  void Update()
  {
    if( networkView == null || networkView.isMine )
    {
      transform.Translate( new Vector3( Input.GetAxis(
        "Horizontal" ), 0, Input.GetAxis( "Vertical" ) ) *
        MoveSpeed * Time.deltaTime );
    }
  }
}
```

This script is very basic. It simply checks if the network view belongs to the local player (or does not exist), and if so it moves the transform with the horizontal and vertical axes (in Unity, by default these correspond to WASD and arrow key pairs, as well as left thumb stick axes on many controllers).

We'll also create our networking script, which is watched by the network view:

```
using UnityEngine;
using System.Collections;

public class NetworkedPlayer : MonoBehaviour
{
  void OnSerializeNetworkView( BitStream stream,
    NetworkMessageInfo info )
  {
    Vector3 position = Vector3.zero;
    if( stream.isWriting )
    {
      position = transform.position;
      stream.Serialize( ref position );
    }
    else
    {
      stream.Serialize( ref position );
      transform.position = position;
    }
  }
}
```

This is the absolute simplest script for networking. It simply sends and receives position. Upon receiving position it immediately "snaps" to the received value. Naturally, this is going to suffer the most in the presence of lag—even the smallest delay will be noticeable, and even with zero lag, position updates will appear jittery as most games send position updates between 10 to 20 times per second. However, it will serve well as the basis for our demo.

To complete our testbed, we'll create two scenes: Our main menu, and our networked scene. I'll name these MainMenu and GameScene.

We'll first create the script for the main menu as follows:

```
using UnityEngine;
using System.Collections;

public class MainMenu : MonoBehaviour
```

```
{
    private string connectIP = "127.0.0.1";

    void OnGUI()
    {
        if( GUILayout.Button( "Host" ) )
        {
            // host a game
            Network.InitializeServer( 8, 25005, true );

            // load level
            Application.LoadLevel( "GameScene" );
        }

        connectIP = GUILayout.TextField( connectIP );
        if( GUILayout.Button( "Connect" ) )
        {
            // connect
            Network.Connect( connectIP, 25005 );
        }
    }

    void OnConnectedToServer()
    {
        Network.isMessageQueueRunning = false;

        // load level
        Application.LoadLevel( "GameScene" );
    }
}
```

This script allows the user to either host a server (by clicking on the **Host** button), or connect to a server (by entering the server's IP and clicking on **Connect**).

In both cases, the game will load the GameScene object after hosting or joining a game. If the user is joining a server, it will additionally disable the network queue, so that important messages do not arrive until the level has been loaded (otherwise, as covered in the first chapter, spawned objects will be deleted upon level load).

Place this script on an empty object in the MainMenu scene.

Next, we'll create a script to spawn our networked object. For simplicity, we'll simply spawn at the game object position the script is attached to. In a real game you might randomly select a spawn point.

Note that we use a coroutine for this. We first wait for two frames, then enable the message queue and spawn our object.

This is because, if we join a server, we've disabled the network queue before loading the level. Level loading takes two frames, so we'll need to wait for those two frames and then enable the message queue.

```
using UnityEngine;
using System.Collections;

public class SpawnPlayer : MonoBehaviour
{
  public GameObject Player;

  IEnumerator Start()
  {
    yield return null;
    yield return null;
    Network.isMessageQueueRunning = true;
    Network.Instantiate( Player, Vector3.zero,
      Quaternion.identity, 0 );
  }
}
```

This is placed on an empty game object in our game scene. We'll also need to save our networked object as a prefab and drag it onto the `Player` slot.

If you run the game now, you should have an example with movable cubes for each player. As you can see, movement of other players appears very jittery. We're going to resolve this using interpolation.

Adding naive interpolation

First, let's add the simplest form of entity interpolation. We'll simply store the position of the object received over the network, and in Update we simply lerp to the new position. This is the interpolation we used in the first chapter when creating the Pong clone.

First, we'll create a temporary variable to hold values received over the network.

```
private Vector3 lastReceivedPosition;
```

We'll initialize this to the current position in Start.

```
void Start()
{
```

```
      lastReceivedPosition = transform.position;
  }
```

In our OnSerializeNetworkView function, we'll store our received value in this variable, rather than directly assigning transform position.

```
  void OnSerializeNetworkView( BitStream stream, NetworkMessageInfo
    info )
  {
    Vector3 position = Vector3.zero;
    if( stream.isWriting )
    {
      position = transform.position;
      stream.Serialize( ref position );
    }
    else
    {
      stream.Serialize( ref position );
      lastReceivedPosition = position;
    }
  }
```

And finally, we'll use the Lerp function to interpolate towards the received value.

```
  void Update()
  {
    if( !networkView.isMine )
    {
      transform.position = Vector3.Lerp( transform.position,
        lastReceivedPosition, Time.deltaTime * 10f );
    }
  }
```

Now, the movement of remote players will be significantly less jerky. However, this method has a number of problems. Using Lerp in this fashion tends to produce what is referred to as "ease-out" behavior: the object initially moves quickly towards the target, slowing down as it approaches until it comes to a stop at the target point (Time.deltaTime yields a good base value, which we can multiply by some arbitrary factor to speed up or slow down the interpolation).

This works based on essentially a percentage of the remaining distance — as the distance is shorter, the same percentage of that distance becomes a smaller value (which results in the interpolation slowing down as it approaches the target). This is one of the easiest forms of interpolation, as it involves zero bookkeeping or temporary variables.

However, it can lead to a very "mushy" feel, especially in a game where players have a high degree of control over their character. We could increase the interpolation speed, but this takes fine-tuning so as to strike a balance between the aforementioned "mushy" feel, and interpolation which is too fast and leads to jerkiness.

What we need is a way to closely replicate the original movement of the player object in a way that looks natural and doesn't need fine tuning to get right. We'll borrow some ideas from the aforementioned source game engine to interpolate our entities.

Improving interpolation

Here's how our new interpolation will work, inspired by the methods employed in the Source game engine:

- As we receive network states, we buffer them up
- Each network state is timestamped with network time
- We subtract a value from time to find a time in the past (in source, this value is *0.1* by default—so entities are always shown one tenth of a second in the past)
- We find the two states on either side of this time value, and interpolate between them
- Let's get started

First, we need some kind of `struct` to store a snapshot of the network state:

```
// a snapshot of values received over the network
private struct networkState
{
  public Vector3 Position;
  public double Timestamp;

  public networkState( Vector3 pos, double time )
  {
    this.Position = pos;
    this.Timestamp = time;
  }
}
```

We'll keep a buffer of these to interpolate in between. Note our use of arrays for this purpose. We use a statically sized array for better performance (if we used a `List`, internally the `List` allocates new arrays whenever it needs to resize, which can trigger garbage collection). This also gives us a strict upper limit on the number of states which can be stored.

When we need to store a new state, we shift the entire array to the right (that is, the element at index 0 is moved to 1, 1 is moved to 2, and so on). The element at index 19 has nowhere to go, and is therefore deleted. We then insert the newest state at index 0:

```
// we'll keep a buffer of 20 network states
networkState[] stateBuffer = new networkState[ 20 ];
int stateCount = 0; // how many states have been recorded
```

And finally, we'll expose how far back interpolation goes as an inspector field for easy tweaking. By default, it's one tenth of a second:

```
// how far back to rewind interpolation?

public float InterpolationBackTime = 0.1f;
```

We'll create a utility function for buffering a state received over the network. This will first shift the array to the right, as mentioned previously, before storing the newest state at 0. It will then increase the count of states recorded, up to a maximum of 20 (the length of our buffer). We'll do this by setting stateCount to the smaller value, either the current state count plus one, or the maximum number of states.

```
// save new state to buffer
void bufferState( networkState state )
{
  // shift buffer contents to accommodate new state
  for( int i = stateBuffer.Length - 1; i > 0; i-- )
  {
    stateBuffer[ i ] = stateBuffer[ i - 1 ];
  }

  // save state to slot 0
  stateBuffer[ 0 ] = state;

  // increment state count
  stateCount = Mathf.Min( stateCount + 1, stateBuffer.Length );
}
```

Next, we'll modify the OnSerializeNetworkView function to buffer states received over the network.

```
void OnSerializeNetworkView( BitStream stream, NetworkMessageInfo
  info )
{
  Vector3 position = Vector3.zero;
  if( stream.isWriting )
  {
```

```
      position = transform.position;
      stream.Serialize( ref position );
   }
   else
   {
      stream.Serialize( ref position );
      bufferState( new networkState( position, info.timestamp ) );
   }
}
```

And finally, we'll perform the interpolation. This involves subtracting
InterpolationBackTime from Network.time, which essentially yields a time
value in the past, finding the two states on either side of this time, and interpolating
between them based on the time. If we don't have enough states to interpolate
between, we simply do nothing—this will result in the occasional hitch or pause, but
can't really be avoided and is present in nearly every multiplayer game.

```
void Update()
{
   if( networkView.isMine ) return; // don't run interpolation on
      the local object
   if( stateCount == 0 ) return; // no states to interpolate

   double currentTime = Network.time;
   double interpolationTime = currentTime - InterpolationBackTime;

   // the latest packet is newer than interpolation time - we have
      enough packets to interpolate
   if( stateBuffer[ 0 ].Timestamp > interpolationTime )
   {
      for( int i = 0; i < stateCount; i++ )
      {
         // find the closest state that matches network time, or use
            oldest state
         if( stateBuffer[ i ].Timestamp <= interpolationTime || i ==
            stateCount - 1 )
         {
            // the state closest to network time
            networkState lhs = stateBuffer[ i ];

            // the state one slot newer
            networkState rhs = stateBuffer[ Mathf.Max( i - 1, 0 ) ];

            // use time between lhs and rhs to interpolate
            double length = rhs.Timestamp - lhs.Timestamp;
```

```
            float t = 0f;
            if( length > 0.0001 )
            {
              t = (float)( ( interpolationTime - lhs.Timestamp ) /
                length );
            }

            transform.position = Vector3.Lerp( lhs.Position,
              rhs.Position, t );
            break;
        }
      }
    }
  }
```

If you test our demo game with this new method of interpolation, remote player objects should move very smoothly, completely natural (past 10 states per second it can closely reproduce player movement even in a fast-paced shooter), and with no jitter whatsoever. But, we still have a big problem—players have a lot of control over their player object. Because players have such control over their own avatar, there are a variety of well-known cheating methods in the hacker community. One such cheat is called "noclipping", named after a developer command in the source game engine, which disables all collisions for the player object and allowed them to fly about the map like a ghost. Another exploit, called N-stepping (for "ninja stepping") or alternatively lag-stepping involves temporarily disconnecting your internet, moving, and then reconnecting. This results in teleporting, as the player doesn't send any move updates for some amount of time until the Internet is reconnected (at which point, the player has moved some distance away). This can easily circumvent speed hack detection, as generally speed hack heuristics must deal with lagging players and can't tell the difference between N-stepping and honest lag.

The way we solve all of these problems is by employing server authoritative movement.

Preparing for server authoritative movement

Before we get started, we'll need to restructure our scripts. We're going to change the Update function so that it isn't called automatically, and instead will be called by our networking scripts. We need to do this so that we have direct control over the exact order in which the simulation is stepped, otherwise we can easily end up with desyncs and rubber banding.

```
using UnityEngine;
using System.Collections;

public class Player : MonoBehaviour
{
  public float MoveSpeed = 5f;

  [System.NonSerialized]
  public float horizAxis = 0f;
  [System.NonSerialized]
  public float vertAxis = 0f;

  void Update()
  {
    if( networkView.isMine )
    {
      horizAxis = Input.GetAxis( "Horizontal" );
      vertAxis = Input.GetAxis( "Vertical" );
    }
  }

  public void Simulate()
  {
    transform.Translate( new Vector3( horizAxis, 0, vertAxis ) *
      MoveSpeed * Time.fixedDeltaTime );
  }
}
```

A few things to take note of: instead of using Update, we've moved our movement code into a Simulate function (which later will be called from FixedUpdate). We've also changed our Update function to store input in temporary variables. This is for two reasons: we'll be gathering input data on every frame. If we sent input with every instance of Update, that would make things heavily frame rate dependent—a game that runs at 200 FPS will have 200 frames of input to send to the server, whereas a game that runs at 30 FPS will have 30 frames to send to the server for the exact same time period. However, FixedUpdate runs a fixed number of times per second—by default, 50. Our client will have 50 frames of input to send to the server regardless of frame rate. Additionally, FixedUpdate utilizes a fixed delta time which does not vary regardless of frame rate. This reduces the chance of getting hacked—if we used Update, we would have to send the frame delta to the server in order for the server to properly reproduce the same motion, making it possible for clients to teleport by specifying a sufficiently high delta value.

This is why we store the input values in `Update` and act on them in our `Simulate` function—the `Input` class does not work properly when called directly from `FixedUpdate`, and in many cases button presses will be skipped.

Implementing server authoritative movement

Now that we have our script structured the way we need, we can go ahead and implement the rest. First, we'll create a structure to hold move commands:

```
// represents a move command sent to the server
private struct move
{
  public float HorizontalAxis;
  public float VerticalAxis;
  public double Timestamp;

  public move( float horiz, float vert, double timestamp )
  {
    this.HorizontalAxis = horiz;
    this.VerticalAxis = vert;
    this.Timestamp = timestamp;
  }
}
```

On the server, we'll store a buffer of move states sent from the client. We'll also keep a reference to our `Player` script for the client and server:

```
// a history of move states sent from client to server
List<move> moveHistory = new List<move>();

// a reference to the Player script attached to the game object.
Player playerScript;

// get the Player component
void Start()
{
  playerScript = GetComponent<Player>();
}
```

Now, in `FixedUpdate` we'll grab the current move state, buffer it, call the `Simulate` function, then send the move state and the resulting position to the server. This part runs on the client:

```
void FixedUpdate()
{
  if( networkView.isMine )
  {
    // get current move state
    move moveState = new move( playerScript.horizAxis,
      playerScript.vertAxis, Network.time );

    // buffer move state
    moveHistory.Insert( 0, moveState );

    // cap history at 200
    if( moveHistory.Count > 200 )
    {
      moveHistory.RemoveAt( moveHistory.Count - 1 );
    }

    // simulate
    playerScript.Simulate();

    // send state to server
    networkView.RPC( "ProcessInput", RPCMode.Server,
      moveState.HorizontalAxis, moveState.VerticalAxis,
      transform.position );
  }
}
```

On the server, we simulate the player, then compare the resulting position with the position sent by the player. If the position sent by the player is too far apart from the position calculated by the server, a message is sent to the client telling them to correct their state.

```
[RPC]
void ProcessInput( float horizAxis, float vertAxis, Vector3
  position, NetworkMessageInfo info )
{
  if( networkView.isMine )
    return;
  if( !Network.isServer )
    return;
```

```
    // execute input
    playerScript.horizAxis = horizAxis;
    playerScript.vertAxis = vertAxis;
    playerScript.Simulate();

    // compare results
    if( Vector3.Distance( transform.position, position ) > 0.1f )
    {
      // error is too big, tell client to rewind and replay
      networkView.RPC( "CorrectState", info.sender,
        transform.position );
    }
  }
```

Finally, on the client we'll receive this CorrectState message, rewind back to the correct position, and replay all inputs from that point on to the current time.

```
  [RPC]
  void CorrectState( Vector3 correctPosition, NetworkMessageInfo
    info )
  {
    // find past state based on timestamp
    int pastState = 0;
    for( int i = 0; i < moveHistory.Count; i++ )
    {
      if( moveHistory[ i ].Timestamp <= info.timestamp )
      {
        pastState = i;
        break;
      }
    }

    // rewind
    transform.position = correctPosition;
    // replay
    for( int i = pastState; i >= 0; i-- )
    {
      playerScript.horizAxis = moveHistory[ i ].HorizontalAxis;
      playerScript.vertAxis = moveHistory[ i ].VerticalAxis;
      playerScript.Simulate();
    }

    // clear
    moveHistory.Clear();
  }
```

We're not done yet, however. Our client is still sending raw position to other clients, rather than the server. In order to implement full server authority in Unity Networking, we'll have to scrap the `OnSerialize` function in favor of RPCs. Unfortunately, this means our entire networking system will rely on reliable messages — The network libraries covered in this book are not well suited to this style of networking as they do not support unreliable RPCs, but for this example Unity Networking will do to teach the concepts. In a production game there are many similar alternatives, which would work better, such as **uLink** or **TNet** as they support unreliable messages. So, instead of utilizing `OnSerializeNetworkView`, we'll create a new RPC `netUpdate`. This will broadcast state information to clients:

```
[RPC]
void netUpdate( Vector3 position, NetworkMessageInfo info )
{
  if( !networkView.isMine )
  {
    bufferState( new networkState( position, info.timestamp ) );
  }
}
```

And, we'll broadcast this from our `Update` function, 10 times per second:

```
private float updateTimer = 0f;
void Update()
{
  // is this the server? send out position updates every 1/10th of
    a second.
  updateTimer += Time.deltaTime;
  if( updateTimer >= 0.1f )
  {
    updateTimer = 0f;
    networkView.RPC( "netUpdate" RPCMode.Others,
      transform.position );
  }

  // [snip]
}
```

And now, our networking system is fully server authoritative, with no client-side lag and in almost all cases no "rubber banding" at all.

Notes on hacking

There are some improvements which can be made here, in order to further protect it from exploits. For instance, the server now immediately runs a simulation step when the user sends input. One only needs to send input at a faster rate in order to exploit this system.

We can modify our server to process input at a fixed rate, perhaps via a queue of move commands which are processed one at a time in `FixedUpdate`. Care needs to be taken to ensure that the server doesn't fall behind when processing user input.

The server could also keep track of the last processed input message, and when a new message is received the server compares the timestamps, discarding the new message if the timestamps are too close together. This could also be potentially exploited if the user tampers with timestamp values sent with the message. You could impose a limit on timestamps, so they cannot be older than a threshold (say, a few seconds), and cannot be newer than the current time (which is physically impossible). Additionally, the timestamp of the last message is recorded and messages older than the last message are automatically discarded. This imposes a much smaller window on hackers in which they can exploit timestamps, and once they exhaust this window they can no longer use the exploit.

Summary

In this chapter, we learned how to apply concepts used in AAA releases to hiding the effects of lag in order to create a better overall game experience. We applied smart entity interpolation to smooth the movement of entities and closely replicate the original motion of the player. We then modified our code to employ server-authoritative simulation for a hack-free game, with client-side input prediction with almost no rubber banding at all.

These concepts are particularly well suited to games utilizing direct client-to-server connections where the server will be simulating the state of the game, and for networking systems that allow for the use of unreliable messages to be sent.

In the next chapter, we'll cover a simple way to remove the need to lead targets in a server-authoritative shooter game: hitbox rewinding.

7
Server-side Hit Detection

There are many multiplayer games which involve shooting at their core, and there will be plenty more to come. These games all need some way to keep in sync who's shooting at who, and who gets hurt and dies. There are a number of ways to solve this problem.

The most obvious solution is simply to have player clients send a damage message. If the player hits someone, send a damage message to the server. The server deals damage to the appropriate player. There is a huge, glaring flaw in this design: players can, and will, cheat the game. It's truly staggering how many client-side hacking programs there are available—programs that send messages to the server, programs that directly modify variables on the client, and so on. A player could easily specify any player to be damaged, and any amount of damage to deal. It gets even worse if the client handles damage messages instead of the server, as the client can also make themselves invincible with almost no effort at all.

Clearly, we cannot trust the client at all, or our game will quickly become infested with cheaters and hackers. Clearly, the solution is to have the server handle all of this—it handles damage and health, it does its own hit detection, and so on. The client almost has no part in the server's work, aside from sending input to the server (just as in the last chapter, we'll have the client send input to the server—in this case, the state of the fire button).

There is one problem with this method, and in fact many games have this problem. When the player sends the `button down` message to the server, it may take some time for the message to reach the server. By the time it does, the target the player was looking at has moved—in some cases, out of the line of fire. This is why many games require you to lead your target if they are moving.

To solve this, we're going to implement **entity rewinding.** Entity rewinding involves storing every network state of an entity—this may seem familiar to you, as we did something very similar in the last chapter. When a player tries to fire their weapon, the server actually rewinds the network state of every entity based on that player's ping, performs the raycast, and then restores the network state of every entity. Essentially, the server goes back in time to figure out where each entity was when the player sent the message (before it reached the server). This allows players to aim at their intended target without any sort of leading.

Client-side versus server-side hit detection

Let's take a look at what our client-side and server-side hit detection might look like. For client-side hit detection, you perform the hit detection on the client and directly generate a damage message to send to the server. For instance:

```
using UnityEngine;
using System.Collections;

public class WeaponScript : MonoBehaviour
{
  public float Damage = 10f;
  public LayerMask HitLayers;

  public void Fire()
  {
    RaycastHit hit;
    if( Physics.Raycast( transform.position, transform.forward,
      out hit, 100f, HitLayers ) )
    {
      // a script on the object could handle this by generating an
        RPC, for example
      hit.collider.SendMessage( "TakeDamage", Damage,
        SendMessageOptions.DontRequireReceiver );
    }
  }
}
```

It's very short, simple, and incredibly easy to understand. However, it's also incredibly open to hacking. Players can easily spoof the damage message to send damage messages to whoever they wish, and they can also easily modify the damage amount to any amount. To solve this, we need the server to figure out by itself who the player hits, and how much damage to deal.

Let's take a look at what naive server-side hit detection might look like:

```
using UnityEngine;
using System.Collections;

public class WeaponScript : MonoBehaviour
{
  public float Damage = 10f;
  public LayerMask HitLayers;

  public void Fire()
  {
    // tell the server to perform hit detection
    networkView.RPC( "serverDoFire", RPCMode.Server );
  }

  [RPC]
  public void serverDoFire()
  {
    RaycastHit hit;
    if( Physics.Raycast( transform.position, transform.forward,
      out hit, 100f, HitLayers ) )
    {
      // a script on the object could handle this by generating
        an RPC, for example
      hit.collider.SendMessage( "TakeDamage", Damage,
        SendMessageOptions.DontRequireReceiver );
    }
  }
}
```

It's nearly the exact same code, the main difference is that we moved the hit detection into an RPC and when we fire the weapon, this RPC is executed on the server. This makes things much more difficult to hack, as players can only tell the server they fired their weapon and the server handles the rest—hit detection, damage, and death.

This does have the side effect of requiring target leading, which gets worse when latency increases.

For instance, let's say we have player A running toward and shooting at player B. This is what the client and server see (approximately):

At this point, player A sends a fire message to the server. Let's say in an extreme case this message takes a full second to reach the server (of course, it's rarely ever more than a fraction of a second, but the effects can still be quite noticeable). By the time the message reaches the server, this might be what the server sees:

If the server performed hitscan now, it would completely miss player B, and even though this is a perfectly explainable situation, it may frustrate player A and even cause them to quit playing, or accuse player B of hacking, and so on.

We can modify our hitscan function to make calls to a hypothetical rewinding function:

```
[RPC]
public void serverDoFire( NetworkMessageInfo info )
{
  // how long ago was this message sent?
  double timeDiff = Network.time - info.timestamp;
  // rewind network entities
  EntityRewinder.Rewind( timeDiff );

  //perform hitscan
  RaycastHit hit;
  if( Physics.Raycast( transform.position, transform.forward, out
    hit, 100f, HitLayers ) )
  {
    // a script on the object could handle this by generating an
      RPC, for example
    hit.collider.SendMessage( "TakeDamage", Damage,
      SendMessageOptions.DontRequireReceiver );
  }
  // restore network entities
  EntityRewinder.Restore();
}
```

So, we calculate how long ago, in seconds, the message was sent from the client. We then rewind every entity to where they were at the time the message was sent. Then, we perform the hitscan. Finally, we restore every entity back to the current state. This way, the player does not have to lead their targets, and overall the game will feel much more natural as a result.

Creating a testbed

Before we create our rewinding system, we'll need a demo game to build off. For this one, we'll create a simple first person shooter (there is a pre-made first person controller asset included with Unity). Players can click to shoot, which will deal with 10 damages to the target. After receiving 100 or more damages, the player is disconnected from the match.

First, we'll start on an empty project. Import the **Character Controller** package (**Assets | Import Package | Character Controller**). This includes a first person character controller prefab (**Standard Assets | Character Controllers | First Person Controller**).

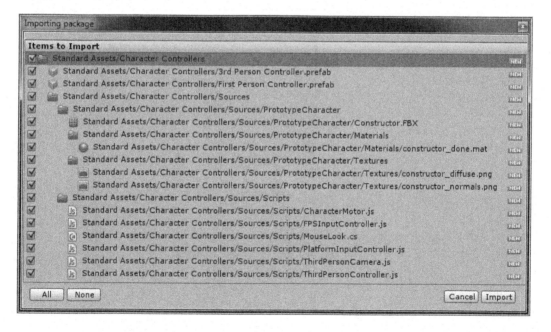

Drag this prefab into your scene. Additionally, create a plane for the character to stand on (make sure it's big enough for several players to run around).

The first thing we'll do is create a script for our networked player. For the sake of the demonstration we'll use a very simple method of interpolation.

Firstly, the base script. We only need three functions here: `Start`, `Update`, and `OnSerializeNetworkView`.

```
using UnityEngine;
using System.Collections;

public class NetworkPlayer : MonoBehaviour
{
  private Transform camTransform;

  private Vector3 lastReceivedPos;
  private Quaternion lastReceivedRot;
  private Quaternion lastReceivedCamRot;

  void Start()
  {
  }

  void Update()
  {
  }

  void OnSerializeNetworkView( BitStream stream,
    NetworkMessageInfo info )
  {
  }
}
```

In `Start`, we'll get a reference to the camera transform, and disable scripts as needed, depending on whether this a local or remote player:

```
void Start()
{
  // get camera transform
  camTransform = GetComponentInChildren<Camera>().transform;
```

```
  // if this doesn't belong to the local player, disable input and
    camera
  if( !networkView.isMine )
  {
    GetComponent<FPSInputController>().enabled = false;
    camTransform.camera.enabled = false;
  }
}
```

In `OnSerializeNetworkView`, we'll serialize the position of the player, rotation of the player, and rotation of the camera:

```
void OnSerializeNetworkView( BitStream stream, NetworkMessageInfo
  info )
{
  if( stream.isWriting )
  {
    // serialize position and rotation
    Vector3 position = transform.position;
    Quaternion rotation = transform.rotation;
    Quaternion camRotation = camTransform.localRotation;

    stream.Serialize( ref position );
    stream.Serialize( ref rotation );
    stream.Serialize( ref camRotation );
  }
  else
  {
    // deserialize position and rotation
    Vector3 position = Vector3.zero;
    Quaternion rotation = Quaternion.identity;
    Quaternion camRotation = Quaternion.identity;

    stream.Serialize( ref position );
    stream.Serialize( ref rotation );
    stream.Serialize( ref camRotation );

    // store values to be interpolated towards
    lastReceivedPos = position;
    lastReceivedRot = rotation;
    lastReceivedCamRot = camRotation;
  }
}
```

Finally, in `Update` we'll interpolate toward the values received over the network:

```
void Update()
{
  // interpolate towards last received network state
  if( !networkView.isMine )
  {
    transform.position = Vector3.Lerp( transform.position,
      lastReceivedPos, Time.deltaTime * 10f );
    transform.rotation = Quaternion.Slerp( transform.rotation,
      lastReceivedRot, Time.deltaTime * 10f );
    camTransform.localRotation = Quaternion.Slerp(
      camTransform.localRotation, lastReceivedCamRot,
      Time.deltaTime * 10f );
  }
}
```

With this code the server now has enough information to perform hitscans: it has the position of the player, the player orientation, and the player look direction (camera rotation).

Next, we'll create the base script for our weapon. This is equivalent to the first naive weapon script introduced earlier:

```
using UnityEngine;
using System.Collections;

public class WeaponScript : MonoBehaviour
{
  public float Damage = 10f;

  public LayerMask HitLayers = ~0;
  // note: ~ [tilde] is the unary complement operator - basically
    it flips all bits of input
  // LayerMask, internally, is actually a bitmask where each bit
    represents a layer - every bit enabled includes the given
    layer in the mask (this is why there are 32 layers - there are
    32 bits in an integer). No bits on (zero) means an empty
    layermask,
  // in the number 0, all bits are zero. ~0 is the opposite - all
    bits are on (and is equal to int.MaxValue). This equivalent to
    an "Everything" layermask.
```

```
void Update()
{
  // if this is the local network view, and the user presses the
    left mouse button, call the Fire function
  if( networkView.isMine && Input.GetMouseButtonDown( 0 ) )
  {
    Fire();
  }
}

void Fire()
{
  RaycastHit hit;
  if( Physics.Raycast( transform.position, transform.forward,
    out hit, 100f, HitLayers ) )
  {
    // let a script on the object handle taking damage
    hit.collider.SendMessage( "TakeDamage", Damage,
      SendMessageOptions.DontRequireReceiver );
  }
}
}
```

This goes on the camera (you'll need to attach a network view to it as well).

We'll also create a damage component:

```
using UnityEngine;
using System.Collections;

public class Damage : MonoBehaviour
{
  public float Health = 100f;

  void TakeDamage( float damage )
  {
    if( !Network.isServer )
    {
      // send an RPC to the server
      networkView.RPC( "serverTakeDamage", RPCMode.Server, damage
        );
    }
```

```
    else
    {
      // note: RPCs with RPCMode.Server, sent from the server "to
        itself" will not work, the RPC simply fails silently.
      // so we'll manually call the function instead
      serverTakeDamage( damage );
    }
  }

  [RPC]
  void serverTakeDamage( float damage )
  {
    // make sure the player isn't already dead
    if( Health <= 0 ) return;

    // subtract damage from health
    Health -= damage;
    // check if player is dead
    if( Health <= 0f )
    {
      // kick player out of the game when they die
      Network.CloseConnection( networkView.owner, true );
    }
  }
}
```

Whenever the component receives the TakeDamage message, it will send a message to the server which subtracts the damage value from Health. If Health hits zero, the player is kicked out of the game.

Finally, we'll create a spawn script for our player:

```
using UnityEngine;
using System.Collections;

public class SpawnScript : MonoBehaviour
{
  public GameObject PlayerObject;

  void Start()
  {
    // spawn the player object
    Network.Instantiate( PlayerObject, transform.position,
      transform.rotation, 0 );
  }
}
```

Attach this to an empty game object in the scene and drag your player prefab onto the PlayerObject slot.

I won't cover how to create a main menu for this demo. You can refer to *Chapter 1, Unity Networking – The Pong Game* for the example code.

By now, you should have a fully functioning testbed. We're now going to modify this to add our server-side hit detection.

Moving hit detection to the server

Our first order of business is to move the raycast function to the server.

We have a readymade solution for this—we can simply mark our `Fire` function as an RPC, and instead of calling it directly, we broadcast an RPC instead.

First, we'll modify our Fire function as follows:

```
[RPC]
void Fire()
{
  // this code should never execute on any machine other than the
    server/host
  if( !Network.isServer )
    return;

  RaycastHit hit;
  if( Physics.Raycast( transform.position, transform.forward, out
    hit, 100f, HitLayers ) )
  {
    // let a script on the object handle taking damage
    hit.collider.SendMessage( "TakeDamage", Damage,
      SendMessageOptions.DontRequireReceiver );
  }
}
```

We'll then send an RPC to call the Fire function rather than directly calling it:

```
void Update()
{
  if( networkView.isMine && Input.GetMouseButtonDown( 0 ) )
  {
    // if we're the server, just directly call the function
    // remember, server cannot use RPCMode.Server, the RPC is
      simply dropped. So we have to directly call method instead
    if( Network.isServer ) Fire();
    else networkView.RPC( "Fire" RPCMode.Server );
  }
}
```

And finally, we need to modify Damage to accommodate our new changes. Note that clients do not send damage to the server anymore, so we'll modify our RPC to work in the reverse — rather than clients sending to the server, the server now sends to clients.

The changes are pretty big, so it's best to simply rewrite the component altogether:

```
using UnityEngine;
using System.Collections;
public class Damage : MonoBehaviour
{
  public float Health = 100f;

  void TakeDamage( float damage )
  {
    // this code should only ever execute on the server
    if( !Network.isServer )
      return;

    // if you plan on calling TakeDamage multiple times per frame
      (for example, Shotgun-type weapons can easily result in
      this), this part is important - it checks if the entity
      already died earlier in the frame, to ensure the death code
      isn't triggered more than once.
    if( Health <= 0 ) return;

    // subtract damage from health
    Health -= damage;

    // check if player died
    if( Health <= 0 )
    {
      // clamp to zero just in case - it looks weird when a player
        has negative health.
      Health = 0;

      // kick player out of the game when they die
      Network.CloseConnection( networkView.owner, true );
    }
    // notify clients of new health value
    networkView.RPC( "setHealth" RPCMode.Others, Health );
  }
  [RPC]
  void setHealth( float health )
  {
    Health = health;
  }
}
```

Note that we simply send the entire health value to the clients now, rather than just the change in health. This ensures clients never have incorrect health values.

Now our hit detection is fully server authoritative, meaning players cannot cheat the system as they could before. However, this still presents the issue of target leading, as it takes time for the fire message to reach the server and in this time the target for a shot likely has moved on.

Entity rewinding

In order to solve this, we need to store the state of entities at every network update. When the entity needs to be rewound, we find the two states on either end of the target past time, and interpolate between them. This technique actually shares many similarities with the entity interpolation code we wrote in the last chapter, and in some places you could potentially reuse some of the same code.

So, in our network player class, we'll create a new struct to store the network state:

```
private struct networkState
{
  public Vector3 Position;
  public Vector3 Rotation;
  public Vector3 CamRotation;
  public double Timestamp;
}
```

We'll keep a buffer of these states, using an array just as in the last chapter:

```
private networkState[] stateBuffer = new networkState[20];
private int stateCount = 0;
```

To store a state, we shift the states and insert the state at 0, incrementing the state count:

```
void bufferState( networkState state )
{
  // shift states
  // the state at index 0 moves to index 1, 1 moves to 2, etc
  // the state at index 20 is deleted
  for( int i = stateBuffer.Length - 1; i > 0; i-- )
  {
    stateBuffer[i] = stateBuffer[i-1];
  }
```

```
      // insert newest state at 0
      stateBuffer[0] = state;

      // increment state count, up to a maximum of 20
      stateCount = Mathf.Max( stateBuffer.Length, stateCount + 1 );
   }
```

We'll store one of these states whenever we receive a state update over the network:

```
void OnSerializeNetworkView( BitStream stream, NetworkMessageInfo
   info )
   {
     if( stream.isWriting )
     {
        // serialize position and rotation
        Vector3 position = transform.position;
        Quaternion rotation = transform.rotation;
        Quaternion camRotation = camTransform.localRotation;

        stream.Serialize( ref position );
        stream.Serialize( ref rotation );
        stream.Serialize( ref camRotation );
     }
     else
     {
        // deserialize position and rotation
        Vector3 position = Vector3.zero;
        Quaternion rotation = Quaternion.identity;
        Quaternion camRotation = Quaternion.identity;

        stream.Serialize( ref position );
        stream.Serialize( ref rotation );
        stream.Serialize( ref camRotation );

        // store values to be interpolated towards
        lastReceivedPos = position;
        lastReceivedRot = rotation;
        lastReceivedCamRot = camRotation;

        // buffer network state
        networkState state = new networkState();
        state.Position = position;
        state.Rotation = rotation;
        state.CamRotation = camRotation;
        state.Timestamp = info.timestamp;

        bufferState( state );
     }
   }
```

Next, we'll create a couple of utility functions: a Rewind function, which temporarily stores the current state and then attempts to rewind to a past state, and a Restore function, which restores the state which was stored in Rewind:

```
private Vector3 lastPosition;
private Quaternion lastRotation;
private Quaternion lastCamRotation;
public void Rewind( double timestamp )
{
  // we're going to rewind to a given position in time, in general
    this would be the timestamp value of a network message.

  // first, temporarily store the current state. We need this for
    when we "undo" the rewind.
  lastPosition = transform.position;
  lastRotation = transform.rotation;
  lastCamRotation = camTransform.localRotation;

  // check if we have enough states to perform a proper rewind
  // if not, return
  if( stateCount <= 1 ) return;

  // check if we have any packets older than the timestamp
  // if not, clamp the timestamp to whatever range we have.
  if( stateBuffer[stateCount-1].Timestamp > timestamp ) timestamp
    = stateBuffer[stateCount-1].Timestamp;

  // network states on either side of the target timestamp
  networkState lhs = new networkState(), rhs = lhs;

  // find the first state with timestamp <= target rewind time, as
    well as the very next state
  for( int i = 0; i < stateCount; i++ )
  {
    // is this state older than the given timestamp?
    if( stateBuffer[i].Timestamp <= timestamp )
    {
      // if the newest state we have is already older than the
        target timestamp, we just don't have enough information to
        provide a proper rewind, we'll just return instead.
      if( i == 0 )
        return;
```

```
        // store the state, and the next, which we will interpolate
          between
        lhs = stateBuffer[i];
        rhs = stateBuffer[i-1];
        break;
      }
    }

    // calculate the total time difference between each packet
    // we'll use this to calculate a normalized time value between 0
      and 1 for interpolation.
    double interpLen = rhs.Timestamp - lhs.Timestamp;

    // calculate the time difference between the first packet and
      the target timestamp;
    double diff = timestamp - lhs.Timestamp;

    // diff will range between 0 (if it is equal to the first
      packet's timestamp) and 'interpLen' (if it is equal to the
      second packet's timestamp). Dividing it by 'interpLen' will
      produce a value between 0 and 1
    double t = diff / interpLen;

    // interpolate between both packets
    transform.position = Vector3.Lerp( lhs.Position, rhs.Position, t
      );
    transform.rotation = Quaternion.Slerp( lhs.Rotation,
      rhs.Rotation, t );
    camTransform.localRotation = Quaternion.Slerp( lhs.CamRotation,
      rhs.CamRotation, t );
  }

  void Restore()
  {
    // restore the player to the state which was stored in Rewind.
    transform.position = lastPosition;
    transform.rotation = lastRotation;
    camTransform.localRotation = lastCamRotation;
  }
```

So now we can rewind and restore a single entity. However, we need to perform this on all entities at once.

To do this, we'll create a static `List` that holds all spawned players:

```
//a list of all currently spawned players
private static List<NetworkPlayer> players = new
  List<NetworkPlayer>();
```

In `Awake`, we'll add the entity to the list, and in `OnDestroy` we'll remove it:

```
void Awake()
{
  // register the player with the static list
  players.Add( this );
}


void OnDestroy()
{
  // remove the player from the static list
  players.Remove( this );
}
```

And now, we can create two static versions of our `Rewind` and `Restore` methods which perform this action on all players:

```
public static void RewindAll( double time )
{
  // iterate over each player, calling the Rewind function to
    rewind that player to a given point in time.
  foreach( NetworkPlayer player in players )
  {
    player.Rewind( time );
  }
}


public static void RestoreAll()
{
  // iterate over each player, calling the Restore function to
    restore that player to the current network state.
  foreach( NetworkPlayer player in players )
  {
    player.Restore();
  }
}
```

Now we can rewind and restore all network players at once.

Finally, we'll modify our weapon script to perform this rewind before firing a shot:

```
[RPC]
void Fire( NetworkMessageInfo info )
{
  // this code should never execute on any machine other than the
server/host
  if( !Network.isServer )
    return;

  // first, rewind all entities to where they were when this message
    was sent
  NetworkPlayer.RewindAll( info.timestamp );

  // perform the hitscan
  RaycastHit hit;
  if( Physics.Raycast( transform.position, transform.forward, out
    hit, 100f, HitLayers ) )
  {
    // let a script on the object handle taking damage
    hit.collider.SendMessage( "TakeDamage", Damage,
      SendMessageOptions.DontRequireReceiver );
  }

  // restore all entities to their current state
  NetworkPlayer.RestoreAll();
}
```

At this point, you should now have a fully functioning solution for server-side hit detection. This can be easily combined with the techniques discussed in the last chapter for reliable, hack-free multiplayer game.

Summary

In this chapter, we learned why the client-side hit detection is very easy to hack. We saw how some games require the player to lead their targets to account for lag. We then learned how we can alleviate this by rewinding potential targets before performing hit detection, so that players can aim directly at their target as expected.

With this technique, in combination with the methods for server-side movement code discussed in the last chapter, you have the tools you need for nearly hack-proof multiplayer games which will boost your overall player experience.

Index

A

arrays, PUN room
filtering 63
available servers
browsing 19, 21

B

BigDB
working with 143, 145

C

chat client
chat room 74
connect screen 69
creating 69
lobby screen 71
chat room
about 74, 76
friends lists, adding 76, 80
client-side hit detection
versus, server-side hit detection 208-211
client-side prediction 190, 191
compiler directives
server console, setting up without Pro 23-
26
using 22
connect screen 69, 71
coroutines 174
CreateJoinRoom method 136
custom serialization function
writing 11

D

custom state serializer
writing 12, 13

dedicated server model
compiler directives 22
servers 22
setting up 22
development server, Player.IO
setting up 128

E

entity interpolation
performing 189, 190
entity rewinding 208, 219-224

F

friends
finding 66, 68

G

game logic class
creating 90-92
GameObject.Instantiate 11
global chatbox application
chat logs, displaying 184-186
chat messages, publishing 181, 182
creating 180, 181
Gravatar
about 187
URL 187

H

hacking 206
hit detection
  moving, to server 217-219

I

interpolation
  adding 195, 196
  improving 197-200

J

JSON (JavaScript Object Notation)
  about 172
  parsing, from PubNub 173, 174
  URL 172

L

level
  syncing, between players 68
LINQ (Language Integrated Query) 64
LoadMyPlayerObject function 144
lobby screen 71, 73

M

Master Server
  connecting to 18
  server, registering 19
  setting up 10
MasterServer.RequestHostList 19
matchmaking
  automatic 65
  manual 66
messages
  sending/receiving 139-142
  sending/receiving, server-side code used
    142, 143
MMO (Massively Multiplayer Online) 8
multiplayer 8
multiplayer Pong game
  ball script 31-34
  creating 28
  field, preparing 29-31

  networked movement, adding to ball 44, 47
  networked scorekeeping 47, 50
  networking 39, 41
  paddle script 34, 35
  paddles, spawning 41, 44
  score, displaying to player 37, 39
  score, keeping 35, 36
  screen, connecting 50, 51

N

NAT 11
NAT punch-through 11
networked levels
  loading 26-28
networked object
  creating 192-195
Network.Instantiate 11
NetworkView 11, 12

O

OnSerializeNetworkView function 12

P

Photon Cloud
  about 54
  connecting to 58
  room list, displaying 59, 60
  used, for setting up PUN 55, 56
Photon Server
  about 81, 82
  connecting to 87, 89
  downloading 82
  game logic class, creating 90-92
  player IDs, assigning 93-95
  server application, creating 83
  star collector game, building 96
Photon Unity Networking. *See* PUN
PhotonViews
  using 57, 58
player IDs
  assigning 93-95
Player.IO
  about 127

U

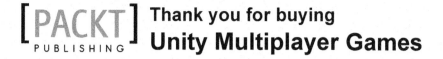

About Packt Publishing

Packt, pronounced 'packed', published its first book "*Mastering phpMyAdmin for Effective MySQL Management*" in April 2004 and subsequently continued to specialize in publishing highly focused books on specific technologies and solutions.

Our books and publications share the experiences of your fellow IT professionals in adapting and customizing today's systems, applications, and frameworks. Our solution based books give you the knowledge and power to customize the software and technologies you're using to get the job done. Packt books are more specific and less general than the IT books you have seen in the past. Our unique business model allows us to bring you more focused information, giving you more of what you need to know, and less of what you don't.

Packt is a modern, yet unique publishing company, which focuses on producing quality, cutting-edge books for communities of developers, administrators, and newbies alike. For more information, please visit our website: www.packtpub.com.

Writing for Packt

We welcome all inquiries from people who are interested in authoring. Book proposals should be sent to author@packtpub.com. If your book idea is still at an early stage and you would like to discuss it first before writing a formal book proposal, contact us; one of our commissioning editors will get in touch with you.

We're not just looking for published authors; if you have strong technical skills but no writing experience, our experienced editors can help you develop a writing career, or simply get some additional reward for your expertise.

Unity 3.x Scripting

ISBN: 978-1-84969-230-4   Paperback: 292 pages

Write efficient, reusable scripts to build custom characters, game environments, and control enemy AI in your Unity game

1. Make your characters interact with buttons and program triggered action sequences

2. Create custom characters and code dynamic objects and players' interaction with them

3. Synchronize movement of character and environmental objects

4. Add and control animations to new and existing characters

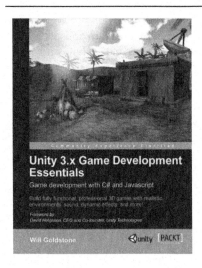

Unity 3.x Game Development Essentials

ISBN: 978-1-84969-144-4   Paperback: 488 pages

Build fully functional, professional 3D games with realistic environments, sound, dynamic effects, and more!

1. Kick start your game development, and build ready-to-play 3D games with ease

2. Understand key concepts in game design including scripting, physics, instantiation, particle effects, and more

3. Test and optimize your game to perfection with essential tips-and-tricks

Please check **www.PacktPub.com** for information on our titles

Unity 3D Game Development by Example Beginner's Guide

ISBN: 978-1-84969-054-6   Paperback: 384 pages

A seat-of-your-pants manual for building fun, groovy little games quickly

1. Build fun games using the free Unity 3D game engine even if you've never coded before

2. Learn how to "skin" projects to make totally different games from the same file – more games, less effort!

3. Deploy your games to the Internet so that your friends and family can play them

Unity iOS Essentials

ISBN: 978-1-84969-182-6   Paperback: 358 pages

Develop high performance, fun iOS games using Unity 3D

1. Learn key strategies and follow practical guidelines for creating Unity 3D games for iOS devices

2. Learn how to plan your game levels to optimize performance on iOS devices using advanced game concepts

3. Full of tips, scripts, shaders, and complete Unity 3D projects to guide you through game creation on iOS from start to finish

Please check **www.PacktPub.com** for information on our titles

CPSIA information can be obtained
at www.ICGtesting.com
Printed in the USA
BVOW04s0049131117

500200BV00004B/34/P